PUB WALKS
IN
The Thames Valley

FORTY CIRCULAR WALKS
AROUND THAMES VALLEY INNS

Liz Roberts

COUNTRYSIDE BOOKS
NEWBURY, BERKSHIRE

COUNTRYSIDE BOOKS
3 Catherine Road
Newbury, Berkshire

ISBN 1 85306 220 0

Cover illustration by Colin Doggett
Photographs by the author
Sketch Maps by Bernard Roberts

Produced through MRM Associates Ltd., Reading
Typeset by Paragon Typesetters, Queensferry, Clwyd
Printed in England by J. W. Arrowsmith Ltd., Bristol

Contents

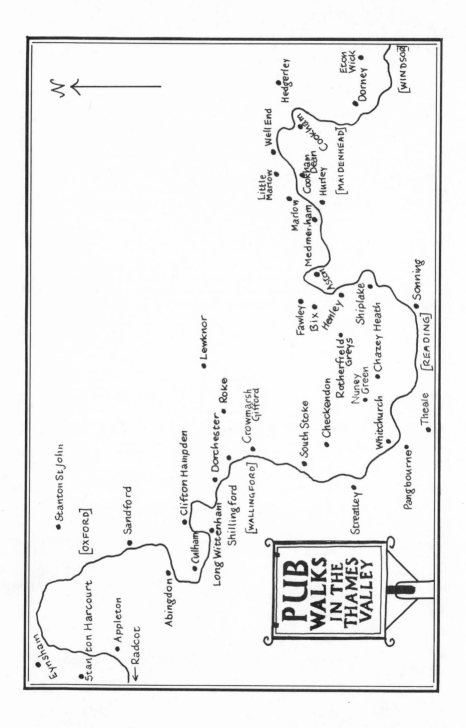

Introduction

Though the river Thames is well over 200 miles in length, these 40 walks have been concentrated in the 70-odd miles of idyllic river scenery between Radcot, a few miles above Oxford, and the beginnings of urbanisation close to Windsor.

The prerequisite for each choice was a pleasant pub in which to enjoy a drink and reasonably-priced food; and, to follow, a walk of about 4 miles in length away from noise and bustle. There had to be peace to enjoy the gentle, uncluttered river scenery, majestic landscapes, wild flowers common to water meadows and the differing plant life of the chalky uplands above the Thames, wildlife such as rabbits, deer and birds, the myriad insects from gaudy dragonflies and butterflies to the humble bumble bee – and the many anglers. It may be, therefore, that the walks appear 'clumped' in some places. Sometimes a charming inn was found but close only to busy roads and in other instances a magical piece of countryside would not have a pub within miles of it.

Before recommending any pub, I have always sought an interview with the licensee to make sure that, at the time of writing, my facts are correct. Sadly, we are living through troublous times for inn-keepers, and the licensed trade generally. So the walker may find that, though the countryside remains unchanged and unchanging, the pub has altered in some respect, though, hopefully, not to its detriment!

Opening hours have been quoted in every instance, some varying from summer to winter. Often landlords are agreeable to walkers eating their own picnics on the premises or at least in the garden, but it is as well to ensure that this is so before unloading the rucksack and tucking in. Most pubs have reasonable car parking and the majority of landlords are quite happy for the car to be left for the duration of the walk but it is a courtesy to ask first! Equally, your dog may or may not be welcome inside or in the garden: certainly he won't be unless he is under proper control.

I would recommend using the OS Pathfinder series of footpath maps when out walking, and grid references appear before each walk description. Summer or winter, some part of some of the walks may be muddy so suitable weatherproof footwear is recommended. Finally, please observe the country code: keep to the footpaths, close gates behind you and do not leave litter.

I hope you will derive as much pleasure from these varied walks as I have found in walking and planning them.

Liz Roberts
April 1993

Radcot
The Swan Hotel

Radcot is a small hamlet on the north bank of the Thames near Faringdon – its greatest claim to fame being that it possesses the oldest bridge across the river. In front of The Swan, between the backwater of the Thames and the garrison field and partly buried under silt, lies an ancient system of wharves probably dating from the 12th century, in the time of Queen Mathilda. These wharves were used for the transporting of local Cotswold stone both to London and abroad to Paris. Taynton stone, as it was known, was used in the building of the new St. Paul's Cathedral after the great fire of London. Sadly, nothing now remains of this trade in Radcot today.

The Swan Hotel is mostly 15th century but parts of the building go back a great deal further and the 14th century stable-block with its charming dovecote was once a chapel. The inn, pleasantly situated by the river, is a Morland's house and, just over the bridge is a 4½ acre island which serves as a car park, a camping and caravan site and a boat mooring. Outside the pub itself, overlooking the river, is a pleasant lawned garden with benches and tables.

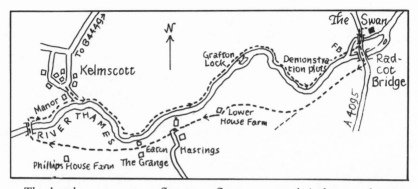

The bar has an uneven flagstone floor, exposed timbers and a vast quantity of magnificent stuffed fish in glass cases around the walls. The landlord and his wife are friendly and welcoming and the food, mostly home-cooked, is quickly and efficiently served. 'Big is Beautiful' seems to be the order of the day and the menu is obviously for those with good, healthy appetites though the omelettes, with a variety of eight fillings, might better appeal to the more dainty palate. There are daily 'specials' listed on a blackboard by the bar and an extensive children's menu. 'Real' ales are Morland Original and Old Masters; draught Guinness and lagers are also sold. House wines, a French red and French and German white, are sold by the glass and there is a comprehensive wine list on offer. Opening times are from 11 am in the morning to 11 pm at night on Saturdays, on weekdays the bar is open from 11 am to 2.30 pm and from 5.30 pm to 11 pm. On Sundays the usual regulations are in operation; the bar is open from 12 noon to 3 pm and from 7 pm to 10.30 pm.

Telephone: 0367 81220.

How to get there: Radcot Bridge is about three miles north of Faringdon on the A4095, Faringdon to Witney, road.

Parking: On the island on the left over the river bridge.

Length of the walk: 7 miles. Map: OS Pathfinder 1135 (GR 285996).

This is an unhurried and gentle walk through water meadows and through the hamlet of Eaton Hastings. After this a slight uphill climb affords splendid views of the sweep of the river valley and the path leads downhill to cross by a footbridge to the opposite river bank to follow it, past both grand and peaceful scenery, along the towpath past the village of Kelmscott, the home of William Morris, and through Grafton Lock back to Radcot.

8

The Walk

Turn left out of The Swan and cross the two road bridges to take the marked footpath, over two stiles, on the right. The path is rough and a bit overgrown in places but it is so beautiful that it is worth making an effort to forge ahead. It follows the contour of the river for about a mile and then goes on straight ahead where the river makes a deep bend. Above Grafton Weir there is a track crossing the path; cross it to a stile and walk over the field to another stile to go round the buildings of Lower House Farm. Carry straight on along the path and through the tiny hamlet of Eaton Hastings where, if you are lucky, the little church will be open to view. Follow the path over a stile and past a very grand manor, The Grange, on the left and then uphill towards Phillips House Farm. Walk downhill again toward the river and follow the path over a stile in the right hand corner of the field alongside a thickset hedge. The path leads to a small footbridge on the right. Cross this and follow the towpath past Kelmscott village. The Manor, the home of the artist and designer William Morris, lies on the left of the short path up to Kelmscott itself and is open to the public by appointment only on certain days in the summer. It holds many of his works of art and is well worth a visit if this can be arranged.

Follow the towpath through grass fields and wide-ranging views with the river side of Eaton Hastings on the opposite bank. Soon the immaculately kept lawns and flower beds of Grafton Lock are reached.

On the far side of the lock the fields are divided up into strips and squares where an agricultural firm demonstrates various methods of farming diversification. There are examples of coppicing, grass planting and sowing with wild flower seed. The whole makes a very lovely backdrop to the peacefully flowing river. The path then meanders leftwards over a small bridge to the narrow road opposite The Swan.

Appleton
The Thatched Tavern

The centre of Appleton village has about it an old world charm; many
of the old stone houses still remain, in particular Charity House Farm.
Modern housing has encroached along the roads leading into the
village which still has a general store, a Post Office, a greengrocer and
a woodyard where garden furniture is made. The church is of 12th
century origin as is the Manor House, moated and still a family home.
The lane leading from the village to the river, Badswell Lane, has an
ancient well known as Badger's Well whose water, so legend has it,
is a cure-all for eye complaints. The Close at Appleton is one of the
houses burnt down to suppress infection during the plague of 1348
which hit Oxford and its surrounds severely. Later the owners took
back the remains of these houses, often just a framework of beams,
rafters and fireplaces, and reconstructed a house of stone or lath and
plaster around the frame.

The 16th century Thatched Tavern was, until 200 years ago, a row of three or four cottages. In the 18th century it was converted to a public house for the use of local thatchers, hence its name. It is, incidentally, tiled and not thatched. The pub has a pleasant red-brick exterior and, although the necessity of providing car parking space has meant that the small garden has had to be forfeited, children are allowed into the spacious U-shaped, timbered bar. The walls are of a pleasing rough grey stone and there are two large fireplaces, one at each end of the bar. There is an unobtrusive computer game and quiet piped music. The landlord and his wife have made themselves and the Tavern very popular in the village and booking for the Sunday lunch of roast beef and Yorkshire pudding is recommended. There is an extensive menu (try the delicious Japanese breaded prawns!), including starters, main course and sweets, all of which are served both at lunchtime and in the evenings. Snacks include plain or toasted sandwiches with a variety of fillings and salad garnish and ploughman's lunches, of cheeses various or home-made pâté. The hot French bread served with this is delicious.

Opening hours are from noon to 2.30 pm and from 6.30 pm to 11 pm every day. The array of real ales is impressive: Banks & Taylor have produced a Dragon Slayer in honour of St George's Day and there is also Everards Tiger and Hook Norton and Adnams Best Bitters. The guest ale is changed fortnightly. There is a full wine list and wines, one red and two white house wines, are served by the glass.

Telephone: 0865 864814.

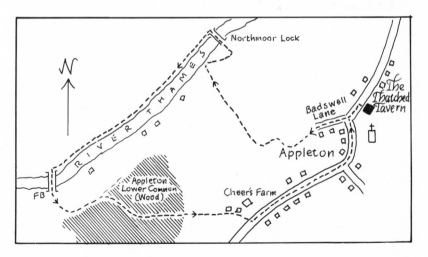

How to get there: The Thatched Tavern stands on the right of the unclassified road leading through Appleton from the A420 and on to its sister village, Eaton.

Parking: There is a small car park alongside the pub.

Length of the walk: 3½ miles. Map: OS Pathfinder 1116 (GR 442013).

A pleasant ramble from the village of Appleton with its picturesque and historic cottages, and including a stroll of about a mile along a quiet stretch of towpath.

The Walk

Turn left out of the pub and, very soon, cross the road to enter Badswell Lane with some delightful village cottages on the left. Follow the lane as it goes straight ahead onto a bridletrack; the hedges are high and, in springtime, full of blossom and birdsong. Follow the track past Badger's Well for about ¾ mile to the river. Turn right here to follow the bank and go over a small brook and a wire fence to the lane ahead through a metal gate in the right hand corner of the field. Turn left and walk across the weir and lock at Northmoor and, on the opposite bank, turn left to follow the towpath for about a mile. The river is narrow and cosy and the walking peaceful and easy with wide open views of farmland on each side and a low border of hawthorn and willow on the other bank. Ducks, swans and geese graze the fields or scramble to the water at one's approach to glide serenely away.

Soon a handsome, almost disproportionately tall, footbridge is reached. Cross the river here and follow the path through a little brake of woodland and over an ancient iron footbridge and then bear left across a field toward the large wooded area of Appleton Lower Common and enter the wood by a gate on the corner. Follow the path parallel with the river walking back toward Appleton village. This is a bridletrack through woodland on low-lying, well-watered clay soil so the walking may be muddy and rough for this bit.

At the fork of the path, bear right to follow the marked path to the wood edge and then follow the gravel track ahead, past bungalows on the left, to the road close to Cheer's Farm. Turn left to follow the road back to Appleton at first past modern housing and then, in the village itself, pretty houses and cottages. The Close is passed on the left and Charity House Farm is opposite on the right. On the corner is a delightful duck pond backed by a high grey stone wall. Follow the road as for Eaton and Cumnor past The Plough inn and bear right at the sharp bend to find The Thatched Tavern on the right.

Stanton Harcourt
The Harcourt Arms

The Harcourt Arms is situated right in the middle of this delightful little Cotswold village, whose name stems from the Saxon Stan-Tun, a settlement near stones. The village is made up almost entirely of thatched-roofed cottages and has a very splendid manor house and gardens which include fish and stew ponds and a chapel in whose tower Alexander Pope sat for two years to translate Homer's Iliad. The house and gardens are open to the public from April to the end of September on the first Thursday of each month, Sundays and Bank Holiday Mondays from 2 pm to 6 pm. The Church of St. Michael is of Norman origin and houses the Harcourt chapel behind finely-wrought iron gates. Here are many monuments to the Harcourt family dating from the time of Henry VII to the present day. On the north side of the sanctuary is the shrine of St Edburg, probably brought to Stanton Harcourt from Bicester in 1537 by Sir Simon Harcourt to save it from destruction by Roundhead troops. It is believed that many of the villagers retained their Catholic faith long after the Reformation.

The inn dates from the early 1700s and is said to be haunted by the

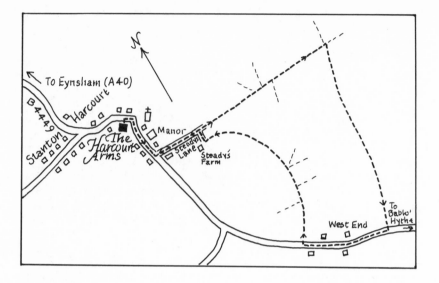

ghost of Lady Alice Harcourt who was murdered by the family chaplain because she refused him her favours. Ghost or not, a warm welcome awaits the visitor. The beamed bar and attractive restaurant are decorated with many caricatures from Vanity Fair by the artists Spy and Aspey, and there is a pleasantly furnished beer garden at the rear. The food possibilities are extensive; the day's 'specials' appear on a blackboard in the bar but there is much to choose from on the menu. Particularly good value and delicious are the baguettes with various fillings including sirloin steak with onion and mushrooms. A speciality of the house is seafood and there is a daily change of dishes. Very agreeable 'house' wine, red and two varieties of white, can be purchased by the glass and there is a comprehensive list of over 100 different wines. There are also good beers on sale, Ruddles Best and Wadworth 6X for example.

Opening times are from 12 noon to 2.30 pm and from 6 pm to 10 pm on weekdays and from 12 noon to 3 pm and from 7 pm to 10 pm on Sundays.

Telephone: 0865 881931.

How to get there: Stanton Harcourt is 9 miles west of Oxford. It is reached along a narrow and winding lane, the B4449, from the little town of Eynsham on the A40.

Parking: There is ample parking space to the rear of the inn and the landlord is happy for cars to be left there during a walk from the village or a look round the manor and gardens, if they are open.

Length of the walk: 5 miles. Map: OS Pathfinder 1116 (GR 415055).

This is a pleasant and undemanding level walk through peaceful pasture and farmland and past some charming cottages and farms.

The Walk
Turn right into the main road from the Harcourt Arms and follow the pavement past the church and manor house on the left. Cross the road to follow the path past a large, old barn and turn left into Steady's Lane. Very soon, at Steady's Farm, the road gives way to a broad metalled bridletrack. Follow this straight ahead for ¾ mile to a narrow belt of trees where another path crosses the track. On the far side of the trees take the marked footpath on the right and follow it, keeping the tall ancient hedge on the right. There are wide sweeping views of fertile farmland on the left and rabbits darting underfoot or sitting bolt upright to survey the scene. Cross three fields along this path and emerge onto a small lane.

Turn right* to walk past a delightful cottage called West End on the right to the second of two waymarked footpaths also on the right and opposite a large modern house. Follow the path over a little bridge crossing a stream and turn right onto a broad track. Go ahead for about 100 yards to a bend and turn left onto the marked path across the field. The path pushes through a scruffy, rather overgrown hedge onto a farm road. Turn left here and follow the road to a T junction by Steady's Farm. Just past the farm turn left again onto the original lane back into the village of Stanton Harcourt. Turn right to walk back past the manor to the pub.

*The walk can be extended by about a mile to include a glimpse of the river Thames, a tranquil stretch running by The Ferry Inn at Bablockhythe. Turn left instead of right onto the lane and follow it, through a permanent caravan park, to the riverside. Return along the lane to continue.

Eynsham
The Talbot

There has been a settlement at Eynsham since Saxon times and it has had 13 different names. Today it is a delightful small town of old stone houses surrounding a square in which stands the parish church of St. Leonard, patron saint of prisoners.

The Talbot is known to be a 17th century inn that probably served the bargees and rivermen when this part of the Upper Thames was busy with commercial traffic. It is built of the local stone and sits squatly below the level of the road, having a warm and pleasant exterior with tables and benches along its front in lieu of a garden. The interior is low and beamed with cool, stone-faced walls which, in the bar, are decorated with horse brasses and a number of old-fashioned prints. On the right of the small U-shaped bar is a cosy little restaurant furnished with wooden settles, hanging lamps over the tables and a huge, black wood-burning stove. Children are able to join you in the inn for meals.

Real ales on sale are Ansells and Tetley Best Bitters and the strong Dr. Thirsty's Draught. Three house wines are served by the glass and there is a wine list. Meals, prepared and cooked on the premises, are served both at lunchtime and in the evenings. Main courses, such as deliciously spicy Cajun butterfly chicken, steak and kidney pie, gammon steak, lasagne and fish dishes are listed on a large blackboard at the back of the bar. Snacks include jacket potatoes with a choice of ten fillings, and ploughman's lunches, of cheeses, ham or pate, served with hot crusty rolls and an ample and interesting salad.

Opening hours are from 11.30 am to 2.30 pm and from 5 pm to 11 pm, Monday to Saturday and on Sunday from 12 noon to 3 pm and 7 pm to 10.30 pm.

Telephone: 0865 881348.

How to get there: Eynsham lies just off the A40 between Oxford and Witney. The road into the town leads to the High Street at a T junction. Turn left and follow the road to a roundabout and here take the B4044 for Farmoor. The Talbot is on the left after about 60 yards.

Parking: The inn has a reasonably-sized car park at the side.

Length of the walk: 3 miles. Map: OS Pathfinder 1116 (GR 442086).

A gentle stroll along the river bank to admire the lock-keeper's garden at Pinkhill Lock, then back to historic Eynsham by way of flat meadowland.

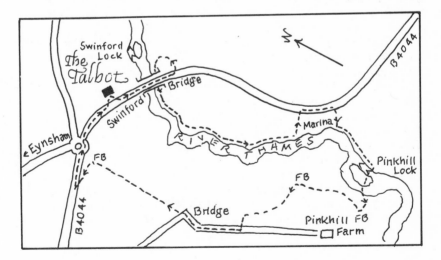

The Walk

Turn left out of the pub and walk along the road on the footway and go over the toll bridge. On the far side, beside a footpath sign pointing in both directions, turn left to follow the narrow little path downward to the towpath and turn left to follow it under the bridge, over another footbridge and on alongside the narrow, curving river bank for about a mile. The gentle slopes up to Wytham Great Wood provide a splendid backdrop to the classical Georgian features of the toll bridge and to the view on the left of the towpath, while flat meadows lie to the right, the river bank laced with low shrubs of hawthorn and willow. Sunny summer days will reveal fields colourful with buttercups and clover over which huge dragonflies hover.

After about a mile a marina is reached; turn left here up the drive onto the road and turn right to walk along it for about 150 yards. Just past a big white house called Woodenshoes, turn right onto a marked path for the river again. Turn left onto the towpath and follow it to Pinkhill Lock where rooks nest high in the trees around the lock-keeper's garden. Follow the 'Right of Way' signs and the clear footpath leading over the weir by a footbridge. The lock was built in 1791 to cope with the commercial traffic on the river and the charming and colourful garden around the lock-keeper's house has been a source of delight to generations of Thames users.

Go over a stile on the far side of the footbridge and turn right to follow a rather faint path alongside the edge to another stile onto a waymarked path in the fence opposite. Walk on alongside the river with a tall hedge now on the left, gradually moving away leftward and leaving the river bank. Go left over a bridge by two stiles and cross the field to go over the stile opposite following the path between high thorn hedges. The scent of the blossom on a hot spring day is most pungent. Turn left on the path at the 'Footpath' sign and, very shortly, turn right onto a metalled track.

Follow the track over flat meadowland to a small bridge. Go over this and, in a very few yards, turn right onto a small path through a thickset hedge. Cross the field and go through a gap in the opposite hedge about 50 yards to the left of a pylon. Cross two more fields, as straight as possible, through gaps in the hedge and bear left to the corner of the next field to go over a small plank bridge by two stiles. Follow the path across the next field to a stile only about 10 yards to the left of a concrete bridge over which the road runs. Crossing the stile onto the road turn right to the roundabout and the B4044 for Farmoor and The Talbot inn.

Stanton St. John
The Star Inn

Five miles north-east of Oxford and high on the stony ridge which forms its hilly surrounding saucer, lies Stanton St. John. St. John, pronounced 'Sinjun', perpetuates the name of the lords of the manor from the 12th to the 16th centuries when the lordship finally passed to New College, Oxford, which still owns much of the land around the village. Across the road from the 13th century church of St. John the Baptist is Rectory House Farm, the birthplace of John White, fellow of New College, later a dissenting pastor at Dorchester in Dorset and the founder of the colony of Massachusetts, New England.

The Star is a 17th century inn still retaining some of its original features: an inglenook fireplace which burns huge logs in winter and a flagstoned floor, now scattered with rugs. The furnishings are attractive, often antique and there are some prints and an oil painting and pewter ornaments. Standing upright in a corner of the lounge bar is the complete shaft for a carthorse, worn and weathered with age. On one wall of the bar are groups of photographs of Morris cars, vintage and modern, and around the bar itself is a collection of about

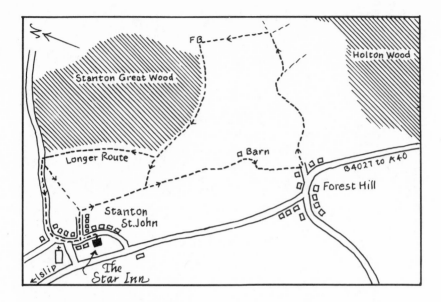

50 brewery ties. Outside there is a pleasant garden with tables and benches, swings and a sandpit. Children are welcome there or 'may bring their well-behaved parents into the family room' which is a non-smoking area down a few steps from the main bar.

Five real ales are sold: Wadworth 6X, IPA, Old Timer and Farmer's Glory, also Hall & Woodhouse Tanglefoot. A delightful and unusual addition to the bar is a wide range of Broadland fruit wines such as gooseberry, raspberry, parsnip, cowslip and damson and a very pleasant sparkling elderflower. Some of these are sold by the glass and all have much the same alcoholic content as an average house wine. The menu is extensive and most of the food is home-made. Two particularly delicious items were the chicken and leek pie with plenty of chicken in a delicious white sauce, and a generous aubergine and mushroom lasagne, both with a pleasant salad addition.

Opening hours are from 11 am to 2.30 pm and from 6.30 pm to 11 pm every day but Sunday when it is noon to 2.30 pm and 7 pm to 10.30 pm. Meals are served every day from noon to 2 pm and from 7 pm to 10 pm.

Telephone: 0865 351277.

How to get there: The Star Inn lies on the south side of Stanton St John and is approached by the village street from Worminghall or from Oxford via the B4027.

20

Parking: There is a large car park, but you may have to look elsewhere on fine summer evenings, such is the popularity of the inn.

Length of the walk: 3 miles. Map: OS Pathfinder 1116 (GR 579091).

A pleasant walk with some sweeping views. Enjoy it at its best on a fine day, when its route along low-lying paths and across some cultivated fields is firm underfoot.

The Walk

Turn left out of the pub and walk to Hillcroft Road on the right and follow it to a gate, taking the bridleway on the right on the far side of the gate. Keep straight ahead, high on the crest of the hill with extensive views on all sides and walk parallel with Stanton Great Wood, a field or two away to the left. At a small barn on the left, bear left across the field corner to cross a stile. Turn right and then left after a few yards keeping the wire fence on the right. Go over another stile and walk over the field toward Forest Hill on the right. Turn left onto a narrow sunken lane from the stile on the far side of the field and follow it for about a mile; there is a small brook on the right for most of the way. Opposite a marked path over a stile on the right, take the unmarked and fairly well-concealed path on the left over a footbridge and follow it alongside the field edge to the corner of Stanton Great Wood, then taking the path ahead up the side of the wood. From the next corner of the wood follow the path on the left to return to the original bridleway and into Hillcroft Road. Turn left at its end to return to The Star.

For a slightly longer walk, follow the path round the far side of the wood to emerge onto the road about ½ mile from the village. Turn left to walk down the lane or take the path immediately on the left and follow it down and then uphill to the corner of Hillcroft Road.

21

Sandford-on-Thames
The King's Arms

The village of Sandford-on-Thames lies on a loop of the river between Oxford and Abingdon, close to the city outskirts but with a rural atmosphere quite divorced from it. The King's Arms is of 15th century origin and much of it was once a thriving papermill. There is a pleasant, discreet development of modern houses and flats in the style of the mill just beyond it, against the lock which runs just outside the pub and alongside its garden. What more pleasant way to spend a summer's lunchtime than to sit in the pub garden admiring the splendid colourful lock garden and watching the river craft passing through. If the children want even more entertainment than this, a large play area is provided.

Inside is a profusion of weathered oak beams, low ceilings and two deep fireplaces in which logs blaze merrily in wintertime. The floors are flagged and tiled, the old stones worn and grooved by the passage of feet over centuries. The traditional 'snugs' have all been joined but are on different levels and the walls are adorned by a variety of old prints and photographs. The furniture is comfortably simple and unpretentious. The pub has its own smoke-room and provides a variety of home-smoked foods such as smoked duck and smoked breast of chicken. The food, very reasonably priced, is listed on blackboards above the servery beyond a long bar counter. There is a mouthwatering display of cold foods – known as 'The Lock-keeper's Lunches' – cheeses, pies and smoked foods and a wonderful spread of salads to accompany these, with crusty rolls and butter. Further along are hot cabinets where you can choose from tempting displays of chicken chasseur, braised liver and onion or steak and kidney pie, all home-made and accompanied by a minimum of three vegetables. In addition, barbecues are a feature of fine summer evenings in the garden.

Of real ales, Courage Directors, Courage Best and John Smith's Bitter are all on handpump as are Strongbow and Scrumpy Jack's cider. Wines, French and German, three whites and one red, are sold by the glass. There is a bar just inside the door to accommodate wheelchairs.

Opening times are from 11 am to 11 pm during the summer months, 1 pm to 3 pm and 6 pm to 11 pm in winter.

Telephone: 0865 777095.

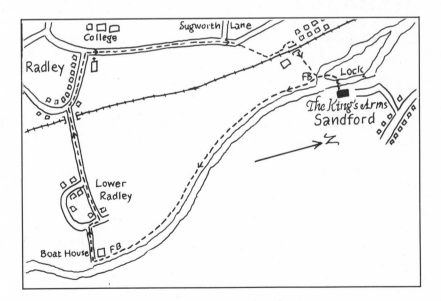

How to get there: Sandford lies off the A423 Henley to Oxford road. The King's Arms can be found in Church Road, a left turn from the main village street between The Catherine Wheel on the left and The Fox on the right.

Parking: There is ample parking space beside the pub.

Length of the walk: 4 miles. Map: OS Pathfinder 1116 (GR 532012).

The views are marvellous beside the peacefully flowing river. The eye can rest on soft, lush water meadows where dreamy cattle graze, swathes of purple willowherb and yellow ragwort in late summer and clumps of shrubby willows overhanging the water. The 13th century church at Radley is fascinating and well worth a pause in your walk.

The Walk

From the pub cross the lock by a footbridge and then over another on the far bank and turn left to follow the towpath. There are low hills to the left and the pylons homing in on Oxford city close by are easily ignored in favour of the river scenes and then, ahead, on the hilltop is the huge grey pile of Nuneham House among its ornamental trees. After a good two miles a footbridge is reached; cross this to walk past the front of the boathouse belonging to the nearby Radley College. Immediately past the boathouse turn right onto a lane and right again at the T junction, walking towards the village of Radley. Ignore the marked footpath ahead, turn left onto the lane and bear right at a grass triangle opposite a hugely tall solitary pine tree standing in front of a handsome old house.

On the far side of the railway bridge turn right and follow the road on the footway on the left into the village. Soon the pretty church of St. James, with its squat tower, is to be found and there is much of interest inside. Cross the road at the T junction to the convenient footway and turn right onto the main road towards Kennington. On the left are the shady grounds of Radley College and, on the right, long views of comfortable farmland. After ½ mile or so Sugworth Lane, signposted to Sunningwell, is reached. Cross this intersection and in about 50 yards cross the main road to take a marked path on the right. Follow this, ignoring side turnings, straight ahead to the railway embankment. Here follow the path as it turns left alongside the railway for 200 yards and then gently down a bank onto a lane below. Turn right under the railway bridge and follow this shady lane back to Sandford Lock. Cross again to reach the King's Arms.

Abingdon
The Broad Face

The town of Abingdon, once the county town of Berkshire, flourished under the benign dictatorship of the abbey founded in AD 675; it was also a busy agricultural centre and a lively market town. Its lovely bridge has carried traffic across the river for over 500 years. From the bridge, the spire of the 13th century St. Helen's church dominates the scene to the south-west while upstream the broad expanse of river and water meadows give a peaceful and uninterrupted view.

It is unlikely that you will have come across a pub called The Broad Face before. There have been many guesses as to the origins of the name. Some say it is the swollen face of a man drowned in the river. Others say it is the equally contorted features of a prisoner hanged at

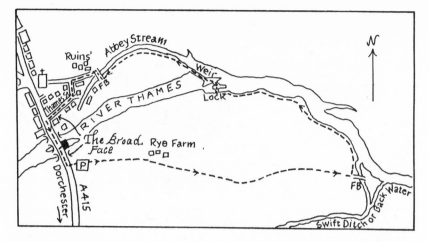

the gaol which formally occupied the building on the opposite side of the street. The answer may be more mundane. It is believed that the pub was called The Saracen's Head at the beginning of the 18th century and the change could simply have been occasioned by poor sign writing – the face on the sign becoming broader by constant overpainting. Or perhaps it was that the main entrance was previously at the corner of the building and thus the pub presented a broad face to the river? None of this really matters, for the present sign depicts a face that is both broad and cheerful, and this suits the pub's present character well. The present landlord is Harry Hunt, who runs it as a family concern with his wife Annette, his son and daughter-in-law.

Their welcome is genuine and friendly, and at The Broad Face you will find excellent, home cooked food. There is a good range of traditional bar meals including cottage pies and curries. There are also steaks of all sizes. For those who like fish there is Dover sole, lemon sole and trout. On Sundays there is the traditional roast – and the helpings are very generous.

This is a Morlands house, as you might expect since Abingdon is the brewery's home. Harry Hunt is a real ale enthusiast and carries a good range of traditional, cask conditioned ales. The pub is open from 11 am to 3 pm and from 6 pm to 11 pm. On Sundays it opens an hour later (morning and evening) and closes at 10.30 pm.

Telephone: 0235 524516.

How to get there: Abingdon is on the A34 south of Oxford. The Broad Face is on the corner of Thames Street, just before the town bridge (A415), on the left.

Parking: Use the public car park (Pay and Display) on the Dorchester side of the bridge. The walk starts from the left side of the car park.

Length of the walk: 2½-3 miles. Map: OS Pathfinder 1136 (GR 500967).

A circular walk from the lovely old town of Abingdon (allow time to explore it) to reach the original stream of the Thames – Swift Ditch – before it was diverted by the abbey monks to favour the wool trade, and back alongside the abbey stream.

The Walk

Take the marked path on the left out of the car park and follow it ahead between flat fields and past the warm, red brick farm buildings of Rye Farm with a constant view, on the right, of the rising, wooded ground beyond the river. Keep ahead along the well-defined path to a concrete footbridge and then take a not very distinct path across the field to the towpath alongside the river. Turn left again and follow the towpath back towards Abingdon to the lock. Turn right to cross the lock and the very dramatic weirs beyond. On the far side follow the gravel path past a new wooden footbridge on the right and on alongside the abbey stream for about ½ mile to another footbridge on the right. Cross this and then turn left to walk through the abbey grounds. On the right some abbey 'ruins' have been reconstructed and on the left is the beautiful Cozener's House. Turn left into Checker Walk, having first noted the perfectly contrived arch which is the boundary between abbey and town. After a few yards the marvellously preserved 15th century Maunciper's House is reached across a courtyard on the left. Here merchants, travellers and guests were housed by the abbey and the maunciper would have been the housekeeper/almoner to look after their needs. In front is the equally well preserved Checker's or Exchequer's house, now the little Unicorn Theatre.

Follow the path through the arch on the far side of the courtyard and cross the road, Thames Street, beyond to see the mill-wheel still visible under the building of the prestigious Upper Reaches Hotel. Turn right to follow Thames Street back to The Broad Face.

Culham
The Lion

The river divides just above the hamlet of Culham to form two separate waterways, joined at Sutton Pools by a weir. There is a fantastic Tudor manor house with massive topiary in the garden opposite the tiny Saxon church on one side of the wide village green while the impressive pile of Culham House occupies the other. The original manor farm can be seen, in its modern day form of small houses, facing the village pond.

The Lion, a Morrells pub, is red-brick, square, turn-of-the-century architecture with no nonsense about it. It lies back from the green, framed by a large tree and with a cosy, shaded garden alongside it, where there is an Aunt Sally pitch and where barbecues are cooked to order during the summer. It is the only community building in the village, apart from the church, so it is very much a 'local' pub, the centre for meetings, games and general getting together. The welcome is warm and friendly and the landlord takes pride in his real ales, Morrells Bitter and Varsity. Two white wines and one red are sold by the glass but there is little demand for an elaborate wine list. There are two bars and a small lounge/dining room where children are welcome to sit; this leads into the garden. Two hundred yards down a public footpath one comes upon the river. All the food is home-made, traditional and very reasonably priced. There are fish and chicken dishes, sausages or egg and chips, steak and kidney pie and a vegetable lasagne, and the local baker produces an excellent crusty baguette which is served with a variety of fillings or with cheese and salad as a ploughman's lunch.

The pub is open from 11 am to 2.30 pm and from 7 pm to 11 pm and meals are served both at lunchtime and in the evenings, the exception being Sunday when the landlord's wife has a day off and cooks only for the family!

Telephone: 0235 520327.

How to get there: Culham lies just off the A415 (Dorchester/Abingdon road) about 1½ miles from Abingdon itself. The Lion is in the centre of the village by the green.

Parking: Park in the pub car park.

Length of the walk: 3 miles. Map: OS Pathfinder 1136 (GR 504949).

A riverside walk, passing an ancient packhorse bridge, to historic Abingdon and back along the causeway above the road. Take time to explore the quiet corners and architectural gems of this delightful town if you can.

The Walk

Turn right out of the pub and follow the footpath alongside it to the right to the river. Ahead are the towers of Didcot power station, a landmark for miles around this flat Thames area. At the river is a

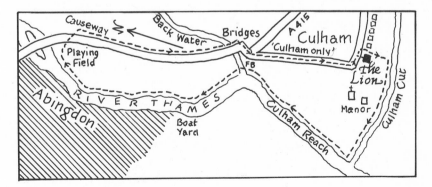

handsome little wooden bridge. Don't cross it but, instead, turn right to follow the path along the river bank. Over the field on the right is the best view of the creamy manor house and the church. There are Barnacle geese and swans by the dozen sitting and 'grazing' in this field! The view extends to the gentle slopes of the low hills beyond Abingdon. Where Culham Cut joins the main river at Culham Reach, bear right to follow the towpath round the field edge. There are many water birds on this wide sweep of river and ahead are the first hints of houses in Abingdon; the tall, slim spire of St. Helen's church pierces the skyline. On the corner of the field the path bears left through a bit of scrub to a wooden footbridge. Cross this and a few yards to the right is a delightful old stone 'pack' bridge, now almost disused as the new road has its own bridge further along. Follow the path ahead over a broad field with attractive riverside houses on the left bank and then a busy boatyard. The gold dome and weather-vane of Abingdon's elegant 17th century County Hall now comes into view.

After about the fifth stile of the route, turn right to cross a playing field towards its pavilion and then on to the extreme left hand corner of the field where there is a public car park. Cross the car park to the busy A415 and go over it to the high footpath on the far side. Turn right to walk away from Abingdon along the causeway, built above the road to avoid flooding, for about ½ mile. At the road sign 'Culham only' cross the road again to take the lane on the right. Follow this for a good ½ mile to return to Culham village past the green and back to The Lion.

Long Wittenham
The Machine Man

Long Wittenham is the site of an Iron Age village and a Saxon cemetery. The name derives from Witta, a Saxon king who settled the area in the 5th century. The village cross marks the spot where St. Birinus converted the pagan Saxons to Christianity by his earnest and enthusiastic preaching! Of more recent interest, a fascinating exhibition of model railways is popular with visitors of all ages at the Pendon museum which also houses a beautifully constructed model of the Vale of the White Horse.

The Machine Man inn, built plainly in 1864, is so named because the first landlord also owned the first steam-powered thresher in the area. He was also a brickmaker and it was he who made the bricks used to build the intricately-patterned bridge over the river Thames at Clifton Hampden. It is, as it always has been, a free house and a proper, traditional country inn. It has not been prettified or done up and is plainly furnished but the atmosphere is absolutely right, as witnessed by the brisk trade every lunchtime when the bar fills up very quickly after 12.30 pm. There is a large selection of wines by the glass from

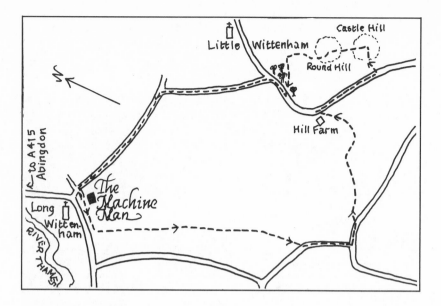

a particularly pleasant chateau-bottled claret to a good house wine. There are six real ales on sale, including Crown Buckley Best Bitter and Exmoor Gold and there is usually a guest ale which changes from time to time. Sandwiches are made of thick slices of bread cut from a fresh, creamy-coloured loaf and have a variety of fillings. Very reasonably priced are the hot meals which include fish, chicken and meat dishes, a vegetarian bean and vegetable curry and a lasagne. Delicious home-made pheasant casserole is served in a brown crock with chunks of crusty buttered bread. On Thursday, Friday and Saturday evenings the little restaurant is opened to serve the chef's 'specials' and on Sundays at lunchtime there is always a roast. Children are welcome in company with an adult and there is a pleasant garden at the rear commanding a splendid view of Wittenham Clumps.

Opening hours are from 11 am to 2.30 pm and 6 pm to 11 pm every day except Sunday when the hours are 12 noon to 3 pm, 7 pm to 10.30 pm.

Telephone: 0867 307835.

How to get there: Long Wittenham is reached from the A415 south of Oxford or the B4016 to the north east of Didcot.

Parking: There is plenty of room in the lane opposite the inn.

32

Length of the walk: 5½ miles. Map: OS Pathfinder 1136 (GR 545937).

An exhilarating walk with extensive views of the Vale of the White Horse, taking in the wooded earthworks of Wittenham Clumps.

The Walk

Turn left out of the pub and follow the track, shortly going over a cross-track to carry on for another ¼ mile to take a marked path on the left, opposite a wooden barn; the path is somewhat overgrown but it is there and obvious when found. Follow the path over stiles and fields with a view of the stubby towers of Didcot power station on the right and the wooded pates of Wittenham Clumps, Castle Hill and Round Hill ahead.

After a mile a road is reached. Turn left here to walk down it for about 300 yards to a T junction. Turn left again and, after about 100 yards, take the marked footpath on the left on an awkward corner. Follow the path over a stile, keeping the hedge on the right and, later, a new plantation in which hens scratch and peck. Having negotiated two more stiles, follow the path along a huge left-turning loop over a field toward Hill Farm house. Just past the house come out onto the road and turn right to follow the lane to a small car park on the left. There are magnificent views over the wide Vale of the White Horse to the right. At the car park a path leads up to the hill-fort amidst the dense clump of beech trees on the top of Castle Hill. From Castle Hill walk downhill toward Round Hill and an interesting plaque which was presented to Northmoor Nature Trust by the AA in 1980 and shows all the local views from this vantage point. There is a short, steep downhill path to Little Wittenham with splendid views of the Thames and Day's lock, Dorchester Abbey, Little Wittenham church and the Culham Laboratory where research into nuclear fission is carried out.

About 20 yards before a gate at the bottom of the hill, take a path on the left alongside a brake of trees and follow this gently downhill to a gate and out onto a lane; turn right to walk toward Little Wittenham. At the Y junction, take the left fork and walk the mile down the lane back to Long Wittenham, making a sharp left turn about halfway along and turning left again just past the 30 mph sign to follow the track back to The Machine Man.

Clifton Hampden
The Barley Mow

The famous and beautiful red-brick river bridge of Clifton Hampden was rebuilt by G.G. Scott in the 19th century. The thatched Barley Mow which lies just beyond the bridge is dated 1350 and is a fine example of 'cruck' or 'crutch' building, a form of architecture whose antiquity goes back to Ovid and Vitruvius.

Mentioned by Jerome K. Jerome in 'Three Men in a Boat' as a 'once-upon-a-timeified' place, The Barley Mow lives up to its reputation with low-ceilinged and beamed bars, the public bar flagstone-floored with scrubbed tables, the lounge with high-backed settles and a series of delightful Punch-like prints decorating the walls. Beyond is a long warmly-welcoming dining room and an exit to the large, grassy garden well-stocked with tables and benches in sun or shade. There are large fireplaces in both bars which burn merrily in wintertime. Children are welcome in the family room which is simply furnished and has handsome squared oak panelling on its walls.

Real ales on handpump are Ruddles County, Ushers Best and Webster's Yorkshire Bitter. Five wines, one red and four white,

German and French, are sold by the glass and there is a wine list. The food, much of which is prepared on the premises, is all of excellent value. There are hot meals, served with four vegetables, such as seafood mornay and various curries, chicken and game pies with generous and interesting salads.

Opening times are from 11 am to 2.30 pm and 6 pm to 11 pm Monday to Saturday and from 12 noon to 2.30 pm, 7 pm to 10.30 pm on Sunday.

Telephone: 0867 307847.

How to get there: The village of Clifton Hampden is nearly bisected by the A415 and is equidistant between Abingdon and Dorchester-on-Thames. The inn is by the river bridge on the B4015 towards Long Wittenham.

Parking: Park opposite the inn.

Length of the walk: 6 miles. Map: OS Pathfinder 1136 (GR 557953).

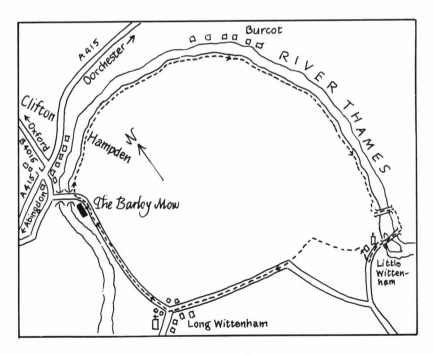

A towpath walk along a calm and lovely stretch of the Thames to Little Wittenham, where there is the possibility of a more strenuous expedition to the earthworks of Wittenham Clumps, before returning to Clifton Hampden by way of Long Wittenham and unhurried country lanes.

The Walk

Turn left out of the pub and return to the bridge to take the marked path on the right to the river bank through two wooden gates. Turn right again to follow the towpath. This is, without doubt, one of the most beautiful and peaceful stretches of the river despite the houses of Burcot village on the bank opposite. Wooden footbridges cross streamlets feeding into the river, Wittenham Clumps stands high above the valley ahead, while Didcot power station looms silently on the right.

After about 3 miles of walking Day's lock and weir are reached; cross the river here into a large meadow on the far side. Turn right and walk alongside the river to a metal bridge at the end of the field. This is just about the halfway mark of the walk and there are a number of options: the walker may like to return to Clifton Hampden along the river, where views are just as beautiful but different viewed the other way; there can be a diversion from Little Wittenham up Sinudon Hill to Wittenham Clumps, whose tremendous earthworks, among the tall beeches on its top, testify to occupation by Ancient Britons, Romans and Danes; or, for the less hardy, a return, described here, to Clifton Hampden over flat meadows and along quiet lanes.

Cross the metal bridge and follow the lane from it into Little Wittenham. The path up the hill to the Clumps is on the left and is well marked. Just past the church on the right is a marked path through a white gate and across a garden, following guide posts to a wooden gate. Go through the gate and bear right alongside a high wall to a stile. Cross the stile and turn left to walk down the field keeping the hedge on the left. The path leads between a group of farm buildings and, among these, take the obvious left hand track which emerges, after about 70 yards, onto a narrow lane. The stumpy tower of Long Wittenham church can be seen ahead. Turn right onto the lane to follow it to Long Wittenham village. Ignore footpaths on the right in the village and, at the second grass triangle, turn right onto a more major lane. Soon the river is picked up again parallel with the road on the left. There is no right of way alongside it here so stay with the lane to walk the ¾ mile or so back to The Barley Mow.

Dorchester-on-Thames
Fleur de Lys Inn

Once an important town, Dorchester was the first ecclesiastical centre of Wessex and the seat of Anglo-Saxon bishops. Today the superb Abbey church still serves the local population, dominating the huddle of timbered and thatched cottages and houses and the ancient inns that make up the village. Within the grounds of the Abbey church, the Abbey guesthouse is the only building to survive. Once a resting-place for pilgrims, it is now a museum which is open on most days. Over the site of the original monastery are the attractive Cloister Gardens.

There were no less than ten inns in Dorchester in the 18th century, many of them coaching inns catering for stagecoach travellers from London to Oxford. The 16th century Fleur de Lys was once the village smithy and bakery and alongside the archway to the old blacksmith's yard, now the car park, is an original 'cob' wall with 'hat and boots'. Beyond it is a pleasant garden with a fine view of the Sinudon Hills

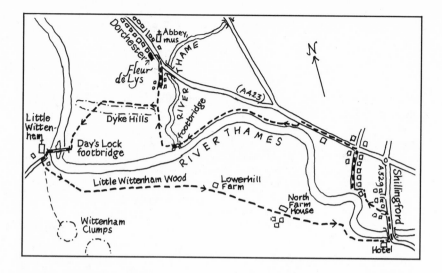

and the Iron Age fort on Castle Hill. Four real ales are sold: the Glenny Brewery Company's Doctor Thirsty's Draught, Ruddles, Brakspear and Flowers, and often a guest ale is included. Good house wines, a red and two whites, are sold by the glass. Children are welcomed and children's meals are provided. The menu of hot meals includes four vegetarian dishes and the day's 'specials', listed on a blackboard, are appetizing and satisfying.

Opening times are weekdays 11 am to 3 pm and 6 pm to 11 pm and on Sundays, 12 noon to 2.30 pm and 7 pm to 10.30 pm.

Telephone: 0865 340502.

How to get there: Dorchester is west of the A423 Wallingford to Oxford road. The Fleur de Lys is at the east end of the village by the bridge over the River Thame.

Parking: The inn has a small car park approached through a timbered archway.

Length of the walk: 6½-7 miles. Map: OS Pathfinder 1136 (GR 578942).

One of the longer walks in this book, but not unduly demanding, unless you want to detour to Wittenham Clumps – the steep way! Enjoy views of the river at its most peaceful, locks, a nature reserve and the opportunity at the beginning or end of the walk to explore the attractive and historic village of Dorchester.

The Walk

Turn right out of the pub and walk to Bridge End opposite a toll-house, then turn right again past the Old Castle Inn. Follow the lane and, just past St. Birinus' church, take the path opposite, Wittenham Lane. Walk between pleasant houses in well-ordered gardens and when they come to an end walk straight on across the field ahead along a well-used path. At the far side of the field is a stile. Don't cross this, but turn right at it to follow the path alongside a wire fence. On the left are the ramparts of the defended settlement of Dyke Hills, a pre-Roman town. Wittenham Clumps stand out high against the skyline. Follow the path as it bears left towards the river and Day's lock. Go through a pedestrian gate and follow the path diagonally across the field and then across the river bridge with a view of the lock and its weirs on the right. Walk straight ahead into the tiny hamlet of Little Wittenham and, opposite the church, take the marked path on the left through a 'squeezer'. For the bold and tireless there is here a splendid ½-mile steep haul up to the top of the Clumps; but for the 'average' walker the path bears a little left and goes over fields and through woodland for the 2 miles to Shillingford bridge. The walk from Long Wittenham in this book leads up to the Clumps by a less steep route!

At the far side of the field go through a gate into the wood and follow the broad path through it, ignoring all side turnings. After about 1½ miles the track broadens out to pass the fields of Lowerhill Farm and then North Farm. Keep to the gravel track and the road as it follows the river down past the Shillingford Bridge Hotel. Turn left to cross the bridge and follow the main road for about 200 yards, then turn left into a marked private road of quiet houses and bungalows set amid shrubby lawns. At the end of the road, at Shillingford Court, turn right onto the footpath and follow it for about 20 yards to a path on the left on the other side of a metal bar. Take this little path out onto a lane beyond and here turn right. Follow the lane right between charming houses and gardens to the main road and turn left.

Walk along the road for a rather noisy ½ mile; there is a proper footpath on the other side of the road and it is advisable to use it. About ¼ mile on past a large Victorian house on the left is the path down to the riverside, through a drunken metal gate. Turn right on reaching the river to follow the towpath back to Dorchester. Go over the footbridge which crosses the river Thame as it joins the Thames and then turn right away from the river to follow the path to a stile and across the next field past Dyke Hills to the stile you didn't cross before. Cross it this time and return over the field and along Wittenham Lane to Bridge End and the Fleur de Lys.

Shillingford
Shillingford Bridge Hotel

The village of Shillingford lies on the north side of the river Thames between Wallingford and Dorchester and the handsome, three-arched Shillingford bridge was built in 1827 to carry traffic over the river to Thame on the turnpike road.

The hotel, on the far side of the river and nestling below a ridge of low hills, is said to be of 18th century origin but has been much added to during this century. The riverside scenery is spectacularly beautiful from the bridge, a wide and gentle curve of water between low grassy banks and clumps of willow.

The large modern restaurant, where luncheon and dinner are served every day, overlooks the river and is attractively furnished and decorated in shades of pink and green. Beyond the restaurant and separated from it by a huge aquarium of flamboyant black and golden fish, is a pleasant anteroom furnished with deep club chairs and small tables. Outside is the terrace where, in summer, garden furniture is set under colourful shades. Up a few steps the two bars are to be found: a long lounge bar, restfully furnished, and the small, snug and cosy

'River Bar'. Flowers and Brakspear Bitters are served on draught and there is a comprehensive wine list.

All food is home-cooked and prepared to order; the bar menu is huge and, as one would expect, a little more expensive than that in a country pub but, even so, it is reasonably priced and beautifully presented. Main courses range from a basic chicken casserole or omelette to sirloin steak with all the trimmings, cooked to individual taste. Huge jacket potatoes with any of five lavish fillings, or a combination of any of the five, are available and all the ploughman's lunches and varied sandwiches are garnished with salad.

Opening times, except for house guests are 11 am to 3 pm and 6 pm to 11 pm on weekdays, with 12 noon to 3 pm and 7 pm to 10.30 pm on Sundays. Children are welcome in the lounge in the company of an adult.

Telephone: 0867 328567

How to get there: Shillingford is on the A423, midway between Henley and Oxford. The hotel is on the A329 on the south side of Shillingford bridge.

Parking: The hotel has a large car park.

Length of the walk: 3½ miles. Map: OS Pathfinder 1136 and 1137 (GR 596920).

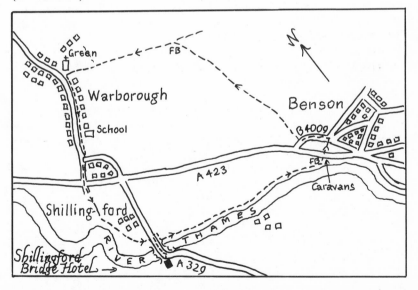

An easy, level walk, partly on the Thames towpath and shared with waterfowl, and then to the charming village of Warborough.

The Walk

Turn left out of the hotel and cross the bridge with care (there is no pedestrian way) to take a path on the right through a small gate which leads to the towpath. Turn left to follow the path beside the river for almost a mile. The water is alive with birds, ducks and grebe.

Just before a large caravan park and marina, cross a small wooden footbridge and take a path immediately on the left between a hedge and a wire fence. This leads to the busy A423 road. Cross this with care to a similar narrow path directly opposite and follow it to a lane. Turn left onto the lane and left again onto the B4009 as for Dorchester. Very shortly, at a wide left hand sweep of the road, take a footpath on the right and follow it alongside a deep ditch and stream. Ahead now is ¾ mile of easy, level walking, a chance to admire the view of Wittenham Clumps. At a concrete footbridge turn left again and follow the track into Warborough with the squat tower of the church of St. Lawrence welcoming ahead. Walk down alongside the lovely village green, stopping at a convenient bench en route to swap maps. When the road is reached, a detour of a few yards can be made to see the interesting little church with its roof supported by oak beams, each pair being made from a single split tree.

On leaving the church turn left to follow the footpath which runs alongside the stream, still in its deep ditch, parallel with the road. There is a delightful hotchpotch of thatched and timbered cottages, Victorian villas and a brick farmhouse on the right and soon St. Lawrence primary school on the left. At a sharp left hand bend, cross the busy road to the path opposite and follow it to the A423 again. Cross with care as there is a blind bend on the left to Wharf Road opposite and follow it alongside the Kingfisher Inn. Notice the 30 or so feet of wisteria-clad cottage and barn wall on the right. At the end of the lane is a lovely view of the tranquil river bank; turn left onto a path about 10 yards from the bank and follow it ahead for a few yards. Turn right to follow the path ahead for about ¼ mile to a lane and turn left with the river bridge ahead. At the main road, turn right to cross the bridge again to the hotel on the far side.

Roke
Home Sweet Home Inn

As the small community of Roke has no shop, no post office, no church and no school the inn provides a very welcome meeting place for the local village population. Home Sweet Home Inn is a free house of 15th century origin; only the barn is now thatched, the rest having been tiled in the last century. It faces the village at a road junction and has a pleasant, small low-walled garden at the front with a well round which an abundance of flowers blooms colourfully in the summer. Inside, the low-ceilinged and beamed bar is divided by a large brick chimney breast with a huge log fire, opposite which is a high-backed wooden settle; the floor is of bare stone flags and boards and the furnishing heavy, leathery and serviceable. The bar itself runs the full length of the room which is often full and very busy. Beyond is a small sitting room of deep rosy-covered armchairs and small tables – a sort of anteroom to the spacious and elegantly furnished dining room. There are several attractive prints on the wall. Well-behaved children are welcomed.

The menu of daily 'specials' is on a board at the right hand end of

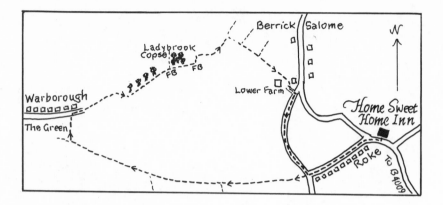

the bar and includes a home-made soup with granary bread every day. Other delicious items include a king prawn curry with rice, chicken breasts with peaches in brandy and cream sauce and sweet and sour pork. These are actually restaurant meals which can be also served in the bar, but 'real' bar meals include a variety of omelettes, give-away sandwiches, plain and toasted, jacket potatoes with lots of different fillings and a huge variety of ploughman's lunches including scrumptious home-made pate and a greedy ploughman's plateful of four different cheeses. There is a large and interesting vegetarian menu as well as fish dishes, game pie and salads all at reasonable prices.

Beside a comprehensive wine list, three wines, a red and two white, are sold by the glass. Of real ales, Brakspear and Courage Best are sold on draught as is Fuller's London Pride.

Bar and restaurant meals are served both at lunchtime and in the evening and opening hours are from 11 am to 3 pm and from 5.30 pm to 11 pm.

Telephone: 0491 38249.

How to get there: Roke lies between the villages of Berrick Salome and Benson and is signposted off the B4009 about 4 miles west of Watlington.

Parking: The inn has an enormous car park.

Length of the walk: 4 miles. Map: OS Pathfinder 1137 (GR 628935).

This is a walk over the flat alluvial plain of the Thames valley, effortless on a fine day, but after rain come prepared to transport some Oxfordshire clay on your shoes!

44

The broad uncluttered landscape is relaxing and peaceful and you can add a detour to the river at Shillingford, about 1 mile beyond Warborough village, if you wish.

The Walk

Cross to the road opposite the pub, signposted Roke village and Benson, and walk down it alongside pleasant houses bordered by a deeply ditched stream on the left and wide views of farmland on the right. The stream meanders along beside the path throughout the walk. At a T junction cross the road to a marked bridleway and follow this well-defined track alongside the brook and out into open fields, crossing a metal footbridge where the squat tower of Warborough church comes into view ahead. Soon the bridleway opens out beside farm buildings and onto the village green of Warborough. It is a pleasant little village to explore and can be reached by following the now metalled track round the green. However, for the purpose of the walk, a cut across the green is taken alongside the hedge on the right and with the swings and slide to the left of the path.

At the far side of the green turn right again onto a metalled lane past houses which soon deteriorates into a grassy 'ride'. After a short time the path turns right to skirt the field and then left alongside a line of poplar trees with the brook, now deep in its ditch, on the right. Follow the track over a small wooden footbridge and alongside Ladybrook copse. At the far end of the copse go over another footbridge, turn left and then right following the hedge along the field edge. Go straight ahead past the metal gate on the left to a stile, well concealed in the hedge, on the left. Go over this and down the field keeping the hedge now on the right to another stile into a little copse. Cross the wood to a stile into a field and cross this diagonally right to a gap in the hedge by a large duck pond. Follow the track alongside the pond of Lower Berrick Farm and out onto the lane and turn left. At the T junction turn right for Roke and, after about ½ mile, turn left to follow the original lane back to Home Sweet Home.

Lewknor
The Leathern Bottle

The Leathern Bottle is of 16th century origin and is just as it was; the interior is delightful with three snug bars heated by a large wood-burning stove in the middle. The stove sits in a huge recessed brick fireplace which had been bricked up three times. The landlord finally uncovered an original bread oven in the brickwork and a 'warmer' shelf on which he keeps, beautifully, half a dozen bottles of good red wine. The low ceiling and heavy beams, plain furnishings, old prints and brass ornaments create a delightfully snug atmosphere. There is a walled garden alongside the car park and children are welcomed both there and in the family room indoors. The huge and varied menu occupies a blackboard above the bar and includes nine meat dishes, curries and vegetarian and fish dishes. The day's 'special' is on a small board and an example is a truly delicious carbonade of beef called 'boozy beef', the tender beefsteak pieces being well and truly marinated and braised in ale with plenty of vegetables added and served with crusty bread. Jacket potatoes, ploughman's lunches and very reasonably priced sandwiches are also included on the menu. As it is a Brakspear's house, only Brakspear ales are sold. One red and three white house wines are sold by the glass; all are carefuly treated and served 'comme il faut' and there is an impressive wine list.

Opening times are from 10.30 am to 2.30 pm and from 6 pm to 11 pm on all days but Sunday when they are from noon to 3 pm and 7 pm to 10.30 pm.

Telephone: 0844 351482.

How to get there: Lewknor lies north east of Watlington, just off either the A40 or the B4009. A sign to the village appears with the road signs directing to the A40 and M40 (junction 6) east and west, under the benign shadows of Beacon Hill and Aston Hill.

Parking: Park in the inn car park.

Length of the walk: 5 miles. Map: OS Pathfinder 1137 (GR 714975).

A varied walk which traverses a little way along both the Ridgeway and the Icknield Way (there is no known language from which the word Icknield derives – its origins are so ancient) and there is certainly a feeling of walking on history as one goes.

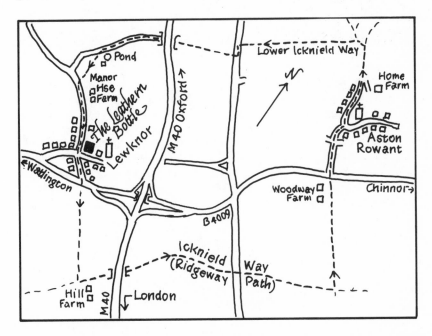

The Walk

Cross the road from the pub into Hill Road opposite and follow it for a short distance and then up a stepped bank onto the B4009. Cross with care to the lane on the left opposite signposted Hill Farm. Ahead, the steep slopes of Bald Hill and Beacon Hill tower above and there are wide, open views of farmland on both sides. Follow the lane until a cross-track is reached just before Hill Farm and turn left here onto the Ridgeway to follow it through the tunnel under the M40 and then alongside the Aston Rowant nature reserve on the right to the A40, a quiet and quite insignificant road nowadays. Cross the road to the track opposite and follow it for another ⅓ mile or so to a bridleway bisecting the wide track. Here turn left again to follow the path past Woodway Farm and across the B4009 to the lane into Aston Rowant village. Behind are marvellous views of Kingston Hill and Wainhill in the distance. The steep, scarp slopes of the Chilterns hereabouts drop abruptly to the flat Oxfordshire plain through which the Thames meanders.

Follow the lane past prestigious modern dwellings and the Aston Park estate to the beautiful little Norman church of St. Peter and St. Paul, standing boldly on a small knoll in the village centre. Walk past the side of the church and on down the lane past pleasant thatched flint cottages. After the cottages the lane deteriorates into a track, low-lying, watery and sometimes muddy. Follow it for a few yards to a cross-track and turn left, then almost immediately left again onto a wide, grassy 'ride' (the Lower Icknield Way) for about ¼ mile to the road.

Turn left onto the road and almost at once cross it to take a bridletrack on the right which is concreted so nearly always clean. Follow this through another tunnel under the M40 and walk on down the lane beyond it. After about ⅓ mile take a marked path over a stile on the left immediately after a small pond and a building. Follow this path diagonally across the field towards the buildings of Manor House Farm. Cross the stile in the corner of the field and turn left onto the lane to follow it to a T junction. The Leathern Bottle is on the left at the junction.

Crowmarsh Gifford
The Queen's Head

The village of Crowmarsh Gifford, on the east bank of the river Thames, derives its name from one Walter Giffard, standard bearer to William the Conqueror, who was granted the land on which it stands. The Queen's Head is the oldest secular building in the village. It was originally a 14th century aisled hall, the sort of dwelling lived in by a man of some means. The elaborately designed timber framing of the aisle and the gallery have been preserved in the bar of the present-day inn which is a free house. It is reputed to have a ghost which was actually seen by previous landlords but not the present . . . so far. Oliver Cromwell is also supposed to have hidden in the chimney recess on the eve of the battle for Wallingford castle, held then by Royalist troops.

There is a grassy garden outside the inn in which stands a terrifying plastic 'plaything' with steps and a roof and writhing arms on which children presumably clamber with enjoyment. They are welcome at the inn and a suitable menu is available. Inside is one long bar and the decor is restrained and attractive. Real ales sold are Bass and Ruddles

Best and one red and two white house wines are sold by the glass. Bar meals, hot and cold, are served at lunchtimes and every evening except Sunday, but there is a regular Sunday lunch of roast meat and all the trimmings with at least two vegetables. The day's special menu appears on a blackboard and there is a printed menu card with an enormous array of grilled meats, fish dishes and at least five vegetarian meals. There are jacket potatoes with five different fillings, sandwiches with nine and generous ploughman's lunches served with a crusty granary roll and a lavish salad. The atmosphere is pleasant and friendly.

From Monday to Thursday the opening hours are 11 am to 2.30 pm, on Friday and Saturday from 11 am to 3 pm and every evening from 6 pm to 11 pm. On Sunday the inn is open from 12 noon to 3 pm and from 7 pm to 10.30 pm.

Telephone: 0491 25082.

How to get there: Crowmarsh Gifford lies on the A4130 between Wallingford and the junction with the A423 (Henley to Oxford road).

Parking: There is ample parking space alongside the inn.

Length of the walk: 3½ miles. Map: OS Pathfinder 1156 (GR 617893).

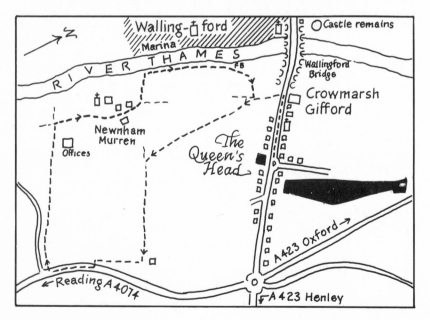

An easy countryside stroll with spectacular open views to begin with and a little bit of towpath opposite Wallingford's marina.

The Walk

Turn left out of the pub to walk towards Wallingford bridge and turn left onto the marked footpath on the left. Follow this to the far left corner of the field where there is a gate. Take the track on the left from the gate and follow it to a farm track in about ¾ mile; the views of open, hill-topped countryside on the left are spectacular. Turn left onto the farm track and follow it to a small house about 50 yards from the main road. Turn right here onto a gated, now disused, lane. Follow the lane, parallel with the road, for about 300 yards to an exit onto the road on the left; walk through it and continue on along the grass verge for 100 yards or so and then turn right onto a path through scrubby woodland over a stile. This is a stretch, a small one, of the Ridgeway path.

Cross the narrow service road for a modern collection of Lego-like buildings, go over the stile opposite and continue along the path. At the next stile turn right and follow the path to the small settlement of Newnham Murren with the tiny church of St. Mary, now redundant, and a large farmhouse on the left. Follow the marked footpath between farm buildings and some red brick houses. Keeping the wire fence close to the right until a large gnarled post is reached, cross the field to the left towards the river and the busy marina opposite. Turn right to follow the towpath with the tall, slender spire of one of Wallingford's three churches on the skyline ahead. The marina and the nearby houses seem to attract a great many varieties of water birds: coots, swans, grebe and ducks of several sorts. At the second gate, by a footbridge, turn right to walk along the field edge beside a brook. Go through the gate at the far end of the field and turn left to return to Wallingford bridge by the original route. Turn right on to the road to return to the Queen's Head.

South Stoke
The Perch and Pike

The tiny village of South Stoke has a large church, St. Andrew's, with some Norman features and a piece of 14th century glass in its south-east window though the church is mainly of later, probably 16th century, origin. The Great Western Railway arrived in 1838, built on a wide embankment with bridges to cross the roads into the village and a tiny culvert, known as the Bogey Hole, through which the path from Little Stoke passes. Brunel's Four Arches bridge, a handsome, brick-built construction, spans the river and the Ridgeway and is a listed building.

The Perch and Pike is a 16th century inn of flint and brick and has a central position on the main road of the village. In its comfortable bar, where a log fire burns merrily on chilly days, are displayed record catches of pike which look fiercely down from their glass cases on the walls. There is a small dining room but customers congregate, for the most part, in the cheerful bar. Children are welcome if accompanied by an adult and there is a garden and play area behind the inn. This is a real village pub, unfrilly, but with a warm and friendly atmosphere. All the ales sold are Brakspear – Special and Ordinary Bitters. House wines, red and two whites, are served by the glass and there is a comprehensive wine list. The menu is interesting and varied: roast joints, venison and hare pie, beef and fish dishes. In addition there are tempting slices of Brie fried and served with cranberry sauce, leek and ham pasty and garlic mushrooms. The ploughman's lunches are hearty and reasonably priced but best value is a giant roll, filled to busting with cheese or ham and a lavish salad.

Nowadays opening times are elastic; it is almost easier to say when the door is *not* open than when it is. Certainly it is open from 12 noon to 3.30 pm and from 6 pm to 11 pm and meals, bar snacks and full meals, are served until 2 pm and from 7 pm.

Telephone: 0491 872415.

How to get there: South Stoke lies just off the B4009 north of Goring.

Parking: There is plenty of space in the car park. However, do let the landlord know if you intend to leave the car there while you walk.

Length of the walk: 4½ miles. Map: OS Pathfinder 1156 (GR 603836).

The ancient Ridgeway path is picked up for this walk alongside the Thames as it makes its way from Goring to Wallingford. A marvellously scenic countryside stroll with a good stretch beside the river. Take time off to visit the little church of North Stoke and the grave of Dame Clara Butt.

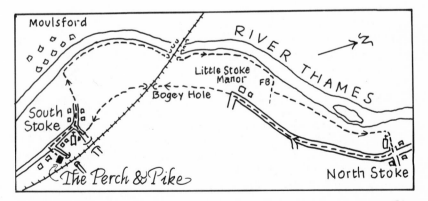

The Walk

Turn right out of the pub and walk along the road past the school and the church to a road fork. Here take the left fork signposted 'Ridgeway' and walk on out of the village past pleasant houses and cottages. Take the left turn signposted to the river at the second road fork past Primrose Cottage and Ashmount House. Turn right on reaching the river to follow the towpath along the bank. On the opposite bank is the riverside town of Moulsford with some magnificent properties bordering the river. Shortly the busy Sheridan Marina appears opposite, near a very small square church with a squat tower. Walk through the arch of the well-proportioned Four Arches bridge which carries the busy main line to the West Country and notice the way the brickwork has been 'fanned' to accommodate the curve of the arch. On the far side is a footbridge; cross to continue alongside the river towards the hamlet of Little Stoke.

After another small footbridge turn right onto a gravel path and, after 50 yards, turn left onto a marked public footpath for North Stoke. Follow the path over fields and stiles with marvellous views of rolling downland ahead. After a good mile the path creeps downhill between hedges to a stile into the bottom of the garden of a very prestigious house with a clock tower. Cross the garden into the churchyard opposite; Dame Clara Butt's grave is on the right just inside the churchyard. The little church of St. Mary is well worth exploring. It is said to be of 12th century origin and remains totally unrestored so that there are some interesting, if almost indiscernible, wall-paintings of this period over the chancel arch and on the side walls. Walk through the churchyard to a lane and go ahead to a T junction. Turn right and, where the road bears sharply left, follow the track straight ahead past Long Reach House, whose magnificent frontage matches well the splendour of the rear and its garden passed through before the churchyard.

There are now wide downland views to the left and ahead. Follow the metalled track over the fields to Little Stoke, bearing left towards the farm buildings and alongside a beautifully fashioned flint wall to a T junction with the road on the left and the impressive gates of Little Stoke Manor on the right. Tucked up into the right hand corner of the facing wall is an elegant brick and stone stile. Cross this to walk along the field side and over a footbridge. Now the field path veers slightly left to discover the culvert, the Bogey Hole, through the railway embankment. On the far side of the culvert the path continues left towards South Stoke again. At the junction with the road, opposite Manor Farm, turn right and then left at the next junction to follow the road back to The Perch and Pike.

54

Streatley
The Bull

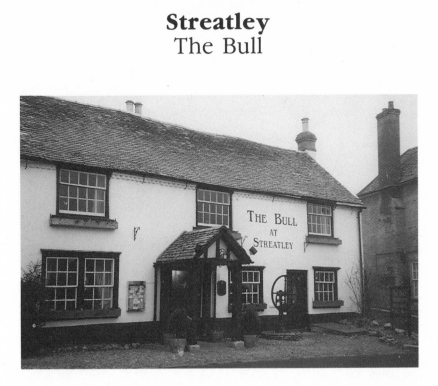

This Thames-side village lies in the Goring Gap below the magnificent, rolling Berkshire downs which tower over it on each side of the river. The village has long been a fording-place, being the river crossing of the ancient Ridgeway and the equally ancient Icknield Way. It was first mentioned in history in a Saxon charter of AD 637.

The Bull is a neat and handsome black and white building with a history dating back before 1440 when stories of naughty goings-on between a nun and a knight abound. Naturally, the inn is reputed to be haunted by these ill-fated lovers! Outside there is a shady and very attractive garden, furnished with plenty of tables and benches and well-used all through the summer when visitors from the rivercraft call in. A warm welcome is extended to children and dogs (if in the care of a responsible adult). Inside there is a huge bar in the centre of which a pseudo-log fire blazes realistically in a deep brick recess, the walls are nicely wood-panelled and the furnishing is pleasant and comfortable. Beyond the bar area is a charmingly furnished restaurant, the walls amply decorated with a variety of

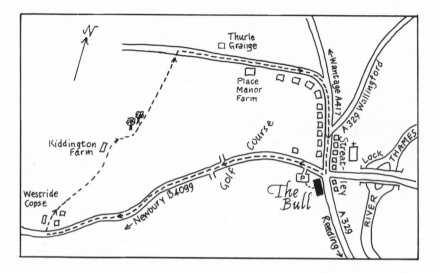

prints and old photographs. Real ales sold are Ruddles, Ushers and Bass and, to complement an excellently comprehensive wine list, one good red and three white wines are sold by the glass. Bar meals, hot and cold, and restaurant meals are served each lunchtime and evening. 'Specials' appear on a blackboard at the back of the bar, together with a good, wide range of grilled meat, fish and vegetarian dishes, and regularly on Sundays a roast meal of meat and two veg.

Opening hours are from 11 am to 3 pm and from 6 pm to 11 pm every day except Sundays when the hours are from 12 noon to 3 pm and from 7 pm to 10.30 pm.

Telephone: 0491 872507.

How to get there: Streatley is west of Goring, and The Bull stands at the crossroads of the A329 with the B4009.

Parking: The spacious car park is a little uphill on the B4009 beyond The Bull on the left. There is a path from it through the garden to the back entrance of the pub.

Length of the walk: 5½ miles. Map: OS Pathfinder 1155 and 1171 (GR 807593).

A steepish climb out of Streatley is rewarded with splendid views over the Thames valley. There is much of interest on this walk, including Place Manor Farm on the Ridgeway and the fine old houses and Norman church of Streatley itself.

The Walk

Turn left up the lane past the entrance of the car park and on steeply uphill on the road for a good 2 miles, past a small housing estate snuggled in a hollow on the left and the toweringly high hills of Larden Chase on the right. The walk levels out after about ¾ mile on the far side of a brake of tall beech trees. At the top of the hill, take the opportunity offered by the entrance to the Goring & Streatley Golf Club on the right to look downhill at the truly spectacular view over the fields and the course to the wooded banks of the Thames some 500 ft below. Ahead there are fine views to left and right of National Trust land, golf course and farmland with a magnificent downhill slope on the right. On a sharp bend in the road, just before the road sign for Westridge Green, turn right onto a marked track and follow it ahead for 2 miles, over open country, downhill through mixed woodland with a deep valley on the left and then along the valley bottom again through open, fertile farmland and past the warm red brick house of Kiddington Farm. High on the hilltop to the left of the farmhouse is a typical Iron Age burial mound or 'barrow' beneath a clump of trees; these mounds appear frequently alongside the Ridgeway.

On the far side of the farmhouse bear right to follow the path along the valley bottom and bear right again at a fork through a scrubby strip of woodland, keeping the bulk of the trees on the left. The path emerges into open country again with a stables and horses in a huge paddock on the right. Follow it to a lane (Ridgeway) and here turn right to follow the lane back towards Streatley. A very impressive mansion, Thurle Grange, is on the left and, soon, on the right is Place Manor Farm, an attractive Elizabethan farmhouse reputedly haunted by a woman in white. There are pleasant houses set high in long front gardens on the right and, on the left, hundreds of pink pigs rootle in a muddy field. At the T junction turn right onto the A417 to walk the ¾ mile back to The Bull, crossing the road at its junction with the A329 to walk on the footway as for Streatley and Reading. Re-cross the road at the traffic lights for safety.

There is no towpath at Streatley but, if time permits, it is worth walking down to the river and across the bridge into Goring. The weirs are very attractive seen from the bridge as is the handsome hotel on the bank.

Checkendon
The Four Horseshoes

Checkendon is a pretty, unspoilt village above a wide loop of the river Thames, and surrounded by beech woods. Its fine Norman church has wall-paintings dating from the 13th century and a 15th century brass in the floor of the sanctuary is dedicated to John Rede, erstwhile Lord of the Manor of Checkendon. On the other side of the road is The Four Horseshoes, a 14th century inn whose original wattle and daub walls still stand in the oldest section. It has a pleasantly spacious lounge bar, unpretentiously furnished and with a huge log fire blazing to warm the heart on chilly days. Beyond is a delightful garden with wide lawns and a play area for children. Tubs of flowers decorate the garden at the front of the inn where tables and chairs are set out and there is a hitching rail for customers arriving on horseback.

There is an extensive restaurant menu with six interesting starters and seven or so main courses including pan-fried fillet steak served with brandy, Cressingham duck and chicken breasts stuffed with asparagus and cream cheese. All are very reasonably priced and served with vegetables in season. The bar menu includes an inexpensive variety of sandwiches, ploughman's lunches of assorted cheeses or pâté, various hot dishes and always at least one vegetarian dish.

Real ales include both Brakspear Bitter and Special. House wines, one red and two white, are served by the glass and there is a comprehensive list of wines sold by the bottle. Barbecues are a feature of fine summer evenings and most summer weekends.

The inn is open every day from 11 am to 3 pm and from 6 pm to 11 pm.

Telephone: 0491 680325

How to get there: The village of Checkendon lies between Henley and Reading and can be reached from the A4074 Reading to Wallingford road.

Parking: There is parking to be found in the pub car park or opposite the church.

Length of the walk: 3 miles. Map: OS Pathfinder 1156 (GR 667831).

An especially pleasant ramble on a hot summer's day as much of it is through woodland. The Maharajah's Well at Stoke Row is charmingly incongruous in this typically Chiltern scenery.

The Walk

Turn right out of the inn and take the footpath on the right opposite the church and school with a sign 'Pig breeding supplies' nearby. After only a few yards, bear left and go over a stile by a gate and walk across the small wood, bearing always slightly left. Cross over a track to a

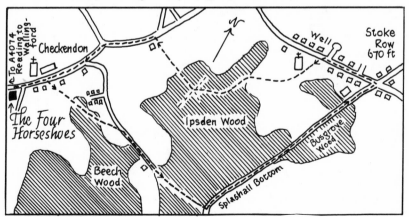

stile on the far side and walk across the field to a lane. Turn right to walk down this narrow little lane with mixed woodland on the right and pleasant modern houses on the left and out into open country. Keep on down the lane past snug farmhouses, ignoring all the alluringly tempting footpaths on either side. At the T junction at the lane's end turn left into Splashall Bottom and walk along this peaceful little lane gently uphill through the densely packed beeches of Ipsden Wood, part of the Chiltern Forest. Suddenly, on the left, is a broad field and open views appear and then a very splendid house, 'Hained-in-Wood'. Walk gently on uphill into the village of Stoke Row.

Turn left on reaching the major road and cross it to the pavement opposite. Very shortly, the Cherry Orchard and then the Maharajah's Well are reached on this side of the road. The well is 365 ft deep and entirely dug by hand, one foot for each day of the year. The expenses of sinking the well, building the little honey-pot shaped Warden's cottage and the planting of the cherry orchard near it were met by the Maharajah of Benares in 1863 as a mark of his friendship with a Mr. A. Reade, a member of an influential local family who had served in India. The Maharajah had the well sunk because Mr. Reade had mentioned to him that his home village had no natural water source. It is open to view by the public, its quaint Indian temple appearance making it a charming little diversion.

After a few yards turn left into School Lane and follow it for a short ½ mile to a footpath signposted 'Checkendon' on the right. The fenced path proceeds across a field and turns left and then right into a wood. After about 20 yards cross a track and bear slightly right to reach the wood edge and cross the stile. Follow the field edge ahead to another stile in the far corner beside a magnificent half-timbered farmhouse with brickwork in a herring-bone pattern. Go over the stile and turn left onto the lane to follow it for about a mile through the village of Checkendon and back to The Four Horseshoes on the left at the end of the village.

Whitchurch
The Greyhound

The sleepy little village of Whitchurch lies on the north bank of the Thames over the bridge from Pangbourne. Its main street is ancient, narrow and winding and is bordered by charming picturesque timbered cottages and houses, some of them thatched. The bridge is a tollbridge, though pedestrians cross it free, and just beyond it is the flint-faced church of St. Mary the Virgin, behind a handsome mill. The main street winds steeply up Whitchurch hill, a Chiltern escarpment above the Thames, below which lie, among other villages, Mapledurham and Streatley; Goring Gap cleaves a deep trough through the Chilterns to carry the river downstream.

The 18th century building of The Greyhound has not always been a public house; it was once the home of one Nathan Bushnell, the ferryman. His wife brewed ale in the back kitchen and it was bought from Nathan by the ferry users. The land on which the pub stands was once the property of Anne, the first Duchess of Marlborough. Next to it is a small building which looks uncommonly like a garage but was the local lock-up where drunks and other disturbers of the peace were left to cool their heels. In 1830 the house finally became a pub and was owned initially by the brewers, Blatch's of Theale. Remarkably, only three landlords have held the tenancy since the Second World War. The low, whitewashed building has a plain exterior but the inside is cheerful and cosy. The one U-shaped bar is furnished pleasantly with cushioned banquettes and tables and chairs around it. There are gnarled wooden beams in plenty but, these days, only 'falsie' fires in the grates; the ceilings are low and the spotless 'offices' are a great trek down a long tiled passage. Around the walls are hung a number of brass and copper ornaments and a delightful group of Punch cartoon prints from the last century. On another wall is a series of photographs of the village and the inn in bygone days and on yet another is an interesting group of signed cricket bats. Children are not permitted in the bar but there is a charming and colourful garden at the back set with benches and tables and this has a play area. House wines – two white and one red – are served by the glass and real ales are Benskins Best, Ind Coope and Wadworth 6X. The menu features on a small blackboard and is not massive but all the food is cooked on the premises: 'We have no new-fangled gadgets,' the landlord assured me. All is extremely reasonably priced and satisfying and the ploughman's lunches, of cheese or delicious home-cooked ham and home-baked baguettes are particularly good.

The inn is open from 11 am to 2.30 pm and 6 pm to 11 pm on weekdays, 12 to 2.30 pm and 7 pm to 10.30 pm on Sundays.

Telephone: 0734 842160.

How to get there: Whitchurch is about ¼ mile from the Pangbourne bridge on the B471 Woodcote road.

Parking: There is ample parking space in the road opposite the pub in addition to some limited space at the front of the pub itself.

Length of the walk: 5 miles. Map: OS Pathfinder 1172 (GR 635770).

A countryside walk of variety, combining splendid views from high above the Thames valley with wooded paths and myriad wild flowers for much of the year. From Bottom Wood back to Whitchurch you can glimpse the river flirting in and out of screening hedges, glinting and winking on sunny days.

The Walk

Turn right out of the pub and cross the road to walk on the footway opposite up through the village. Cross again at the top of the village to make use of the conveniently raised grass verge as far as the war memorial. Cross the road once again at the memorial and, just past a large house called Stoneycroft, take the path on the left and go over a stile ahead. Follow the path on the left along the side of the field with woodland falling away to the left. At the end of the field, follow footpath signs through a fenced grass track alongside Beech Farm buildings. Just past the end of the buildings, take the path on the left alongside a grass field. At the top of the field, don't go through the gate into the wood but instead turn right to walk across the field edge with the wood on the left to a barred exit and a kissing gate in the left hand corner. Here the concrete drive to the farm is picked up again. Turn left to take it to the road, the B471, and cross with care, then turn right to pass the front of the church of St. John the Baptist.

Just past the church turn left to cross the green to a metal gate onto a lane. Turn right again and very soon cross the lane to a marked footpath with fencing on each side. After going through a gate, keep to the obvious path very slightly uphill and leftward towards the left hand end of a group of trees on the horizon. Go through another gate onto a farm track and follow this straight ahead and slightly downhill

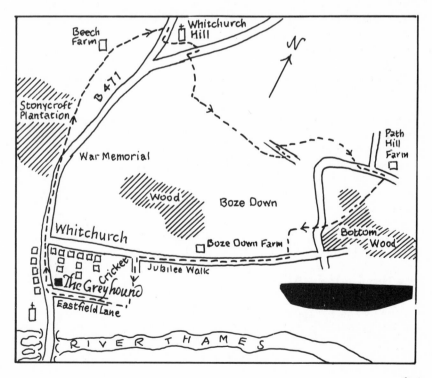

past a busy pig farm. At a path junction by a line of trees bear right to follow the field edge downhill keeping the hedge on the right. The path descends, over an awkward stile, to a narrow lane. Here turn left and, after about 50 yards, turn right again over a stile onto a marked footpath along the field edge, keeping the hedge, this time, on the left. Go over yet another awkward stile at the end of the field onto a short track up to a lane and keep left. Where the lane makes an abrupt left turn, take the winding lane on the right and follow it to Path Hill Farm. Turn right onto the public footpath immediately before Path Hill Farm's farm shop. Follow the path past The Baulk, an amazing house with two tall turrets at its front, and go on downhill on a narrowing path between hedges, brilliantly colourful with wild flowers in summer and autumn, into Bottom Wood, a carpet of bluebells in the spring. The path descends to a lane; cross this to a path on the far side and follow it, keeping the hedge on the left. There are magnificent views here: the tall, undulating roll of Boze Down towering up on the right and the flat meadows going down to the Thames bank on the left.

After going through a gate at the end of the field, turn left to walk downhill gently alongside the hedge to the lane at the bottom. Go through the gate and then turn right onto the lane, walking on the grass verge and, after the buildings of Boze Farm, up onto the raised Jubilee Walk. This walk, above the lane and shaded by an overhang of small trees, was fashioned to commemorate the Queen's Jubilee in 1977 and there is a seat to prove it halfway along. About 100 yards past the Whitchurch-on-Thames sign on the left, turn down off the Jubilee Walk via some rather dodgy wooden steps on the left and cross the lane to a gravel track to follow it past allotments and the cricket ground. At the end of the cricket ground turn right and keep right onto Eastfield Lane to return to The Greyhound, standing on the right hand corner of the lane.

Pangbourne
The Cross Keys

The village of Pangbourne lies where the river Thames meets with the tiny river Pang and it was here that the ancient Ridgeway dropped down into the valley from Basildon to cross, first by ford, and later, by a rough bridge. Among a row of well-preserved 16th and 17th century cottages opposite the church, is The Cross Keys whose main building is of 16th century origin; low-ceilinged, small rooms, heavily beamed. There are two bars and a family room with appropriate small furnishings for the children. The house has a cheerful and welcoming atmosphere. Behind the pub is a pleasant patio area bounded by the Pang at the end.

Three French house wines are served and there is an adequate wine list. Real ales sold are Courage Best and Courage Directors and Eldridge Pope Thomas Hardy.

Most of the food, steaks and mixed grills excepted, is ridiculously cheap and uniformly excellent. There's home-made soup, home-baked ham, fish and chicken dishes and a vegetarian quiche, as well as lavish salads and all the usual bar meals.

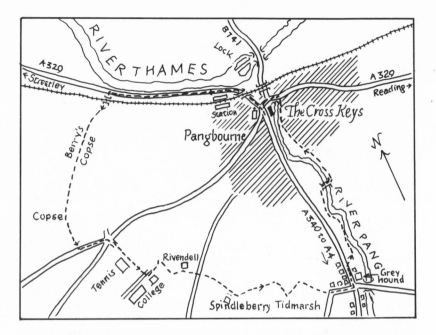

Opening hours are from 11 am to 3 pm and from 6 pm to 11 pm on all days except Sundays when hours are from 12 pm to 3 pm and 7 pm to 10.30 pm. Food is served at lunchtime and in the evening. Telephone: 0734 843268.

How to get there: The village lies on the south bank of the Thames, where the B471 from Woodcote meets the A329 (Reading road) and the A340 running northwards from Basingstoke.

Parking: Park in the public car park in Station Road, just past the inn, off St. James Close on the left and opposite the Lancaster Garage.

Length of the walk: 5½ miles. Map: OS Pathfinder 1172 (GR 635765).

This route will give you broad river views as you walk beside the Thames west of Pangbourne and, later, the contrasting delights of the little Pang.

The Walk
Turn right out of the pub and walk ahead along Station Road and under the railway bridge following the road beyond, Shooter Hill, After about a mile at a bus stop, cross the road to take the marked path

66

on the left under another railway bridge. Turn left on the far side of the bridge to follow the winding path gently uphill. Follow the path across this treeless area to enter a beechwood, Berry's Copse, and go on to a metal kissing gate. Through the gate bear left to walk along a broad ride with a hedge on the left and, at the next gate, cross the field ahead diagonally towards an obvious gap in the trees at the corner of a copse on the right. Go through the gap and bear left to follow a track to a lane. Go through a gate and turn left to follow this quite busy little lane to a junction with a more major road. Cross the road to a narrow lane opposite signposted to Pangbourne College.

Walk past the college tennis courts on the right and, at the estate road, turn left and after 100 yards turn right onto a gravel track between No Through Way notices. Bear left to follow the gravel track ahead and gently downhill, ignoring the school path on the extreme left. Walk past a pleasant house called 'Rivendell' and on to a lane at the bottom of the hill. Cross the lane to the track opposite and follow it ahead to an isolated house called 'Spindleberry' on the right and enter a narrow, hedged path bearing left.

Follow the path as it bears right at the field end with the hedge on the left and then left at the next corner with the hedge now on the right. Soon there is another sharp bend to the right and a short, steep climb to a metal gate and stile and then downhill to the lane on the far side of the farm ahead. Turn left onto the lane and then left again, onto the main road opposite The Greyhound Inn at Tidmarsh. When the footway on the left runs out, cross the road and take the marked path on the right into a field and then along the side and back of a pleasant garden. Follow the narrow little path as it winds its way toward the river Pang on the right and on past a house called 'Longbridge'. Emerge onto the drive of Longbridge on the right and turn left to follow the gravel track ahead which is signposted with the names of three houses. At the end of the track go over the two stiles on either side of the field and follow the path alongside the narrow river bank. Go over a footbridge and follow the bank on the far side and across a field to a wooden gate to the right of the river. Go through the gate to follow a shady path behind houses onto a lane between houses, The Moors. Emerge onto the Reading road and turn left to walk up to Station Road and the car park on the far side.

Theale
The Gathering

There are six pubs in the main street of Theale but in the high days of coaching inns there were many more. Theale was nicknamed 'Little Sodom' then! It remained a bustling little village on the busy A4, London to Bath, road until the arrival of the M4 motorway. Now it lies quietly reposing in a slip-road, bypassed by the roaring traffic so near it on the M4.

The Gathering, a delightful early 18th century building of character and charm, lies at the east end of the High Street. It boasts a large horse-shoe shaped bar surrounded by dark wood furniture and above is a delightful restaurant with an unrestricted view of the old High Street from the wide casement windows giving the whole room a light, airy feeling about it. There is a magnificent criss-cross of exposed beams and a fire blazes merrily on cold days.

Downstairs in the bar Ansell's and Tetley's Bitter are both served on hand-pump as is Castlemaine XXXX lager. Three very drinkable house wines are on offer, one red and two white, and there is an extensive wine list from which to choose. Varieties of coffee were available and a pot of tea could be had at any time. The food is varied and not expensive: jacket potatoes, salad platters and ploughman's lunches of cheeses or pâté, served with salad and an apple, and (considered by me as excellent value) an enormous wholemeal bap, filled to bursting with either prawns and cheese, chicken tikka and apple, ham and tomato or cheese and pickle. A blackboard listed the day's specials – chilli con carne and a vegetarian lasagne when we were there.

In the summertime, tables and chairs are set in the sun under umbrellas along the paved side of the bar. Opening hours are from 11 am to 11 pm and on Sunday, 12 noon to 3 pm and 7 pm to 10.30 pm. Well-behaved children are welcomed under supervision. The restaurant is open 12 noon to 2.30 pm and 7 pm to 10 pm and is closed on Sundays.

Telephone: 0734 303478.

How to get there: Leave the M4 at exit 12 for Theale and take the turning marked 'High Street Only'. At the roundabout turn left. The Gathering Restaurant/Bar is about 20 yards ahead on the right.

Parking: There is ample car parking close to the house and ahead a huge, gravelled overflow car parking space.

Length of the walk: 3 miles. Map: OS Pathfinder 1172 (GR 640713).

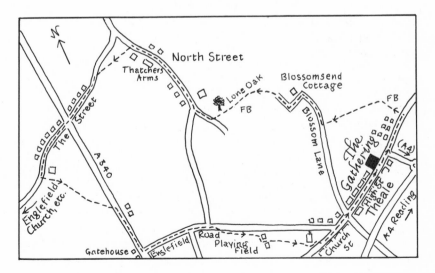

This is a gentle three miles over flat countryside through the edges of the delightful little hamlets of North Street and Englefield.

The Walk

Turn left out of the bar to walk down the High Street and, just past the last house of a small housing estate on the left, take the marked path on the left and follow it over a footbridge across a stream. Here turn left again onto a path at the field edge with the spired tower of Theale's huge church of the Holy Trinity on the left. Follow the path across the middle of the field to Blossom Lane where you then turn right. At the end of the lane turn left onto a path just by Blossomsend Cottage and follow this grassy path between hedges to a stile. Over the stile bear slightly left across the field past a squat, single oak tree on the right and on to another stile.

Over the stile turn right onto a metalled path and follow it to the road where you then turn right again to follow the lane through North Street and past The Thatchers Arms on the left. Just past The Grange take the marked path on the left across the middle of a field and alongside the hedge on the left to a stile emerging onto a lane. Turn left onto the lane and follow it to the main road (A340 to Pangbourne) which you must cross with care to continue along the lane, now called The Street, past charming red brick estate cottages on the right and shortly, a large detached house just beyond which is a public footpath sign pointing left.

Ahead lies the pleasant village of Englefield but to continue the walk, return to the large house, now on the right, with its pleasant and well-kept garden and take the marked path on the right immediately before it running alongside the garden and through a metal gate. Cross two stiles on either side of a small field and, after the second one, go slightly left across the next, larger grass field to a stile emerging onto the main road again. Turn right onto the road and, keeping to the grass verge, follow it for a rather traffic-beset 200 yards.

Opposite the ornate gatehouse to the Englefield Estate, cross the main road to go down the one opposite, Englefield Road. Go past the school playing field on the right, with its pavilion at the far end. After the social club on the right, walk across the recreation ground on the other side to the edge of the churchyard near the children's play area. Follow the path which runs straight through the middle of the churchyard keeping the tall stone edifice on the left. Turn left past the church and right under the arch toward Church Street. Turn left here and follow Church Street and High Street back to The Gathering.

70

Goring Heath
The King Charles Head

The King Charles Head was converted earlier this century from a game-keeper's cottage and is a free house. It lies on the B4526, Goring Heath road, off the A4074 from Reading to Wallingford.

There are two bars; a well, but plainly, furnished public bar and a more comfortable lounge bar with a small restaurant off it. The walls of both the bars are pleasingly decorated with vintage china plates depicting a variety of sporting events. There is a roaring log fire in a deeply recessed fireplace on chilly days. Outside is a huge lawned garden backed by woodland and with some handsome specimen trees in it. It is furnished with wooden tables and benches and there is a children's play area. Barbecues are prepared in the garden on sunny summer evenings. Opening hours are from 10.30 am to 2.30 pm and from 6 pm to 11 pm on weekdays and from noon to 3 pm and 7 pm to 10.30 pm on Sunday. Well-behaved children are permitted in the bars, dogs only in the public bar and no muddy boots anywhere by request of the landlord. Food is served in the bar and restaurant from 12 pm to 2 pm and 7pm to 9 pm.

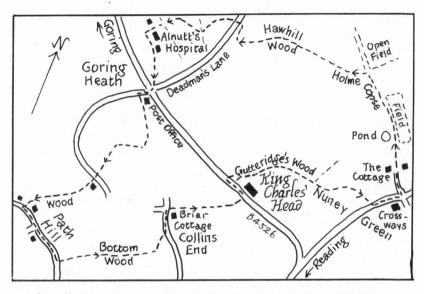

Of 'real' ales there is a wide choice: Brakspear's Best, Boddingtons and Flowers and Wadworth 6X all on hand-pump as are lagers and Scrumpy Jack cider. There are twelve house wines which can be purchased by the glass and a comprehensive wine list in addition. Two large boards, one in each bar, display the bar food 'specials' for the day, all food served is excellent value, home-cooked and varied with a good variety of vegetarian dishes. 'Dish of the Day' was hearty helpings of a truly delicious hot game pie (it was hare on our visit).

Telephone: 0491 680268.

How to get there: Turn off the A4074, Reading to Wallingford road onto the B4526. The King Charles Head lies on your right, before you reach the village of Goring Heath itself.

Parking: A large car park runs the length of the pub's side and there is parking at the front and in the lane opposite.

Length of the walk: 4 miles. Map: OS Pathfinder 1172 (GR 664788).

Just a few miles north west of the large and busy county town of Reading lies magnificent, peaceful countryside with panoramic views toward the Thames valley and beautiful stands of beech wood. There are three small hamlets on the route of the walk and the equine population encountered (kept within fenced paddocks!) almost outnumbers the human.

The Walk

Much of the walk is through woodland and walking shoes are recommended for those inevitable muddy patches at any time of year. The paths on the route are well-defined by white arrows painted on the trees so keep an eye open for them to lead you through.

Turn right out of the pub and walk down the road for about 150 yards then take the waymarked bridleway on the right through Gutteridge's Wood for about ½ mile, bearing slightly right at a Y junction in the track.

The track emerges onto a metalled lane; turn left here to walk up the lane to a bungalow on the right called Crossways where you turn left again along the track and then, between two delightful thatched cottages, Straw Eaves and The Cottage, follow a narrow, hedged path into the wood ahead, following the white arrows which define the path. At the wood edge bear left to go round a small pond, keeping a long, narrow open field on the right and then a wire fence. At a clearly marked cross-path at the corner of a large open field, bear ½ left along a waymarked woodland path through Holme Copse and Hawhill Wood for about 150 yards where, at another cross-path, go over the cross and bear slightly right to keep a long squat earth bank on the left and still following the arrows on the trees.

After a collection of rather muddy intersections where forestry work has been in progress, the waymarked path narrows and goes gently downhill through the wood to a field edge where you bear right to follow the path along the wood edge to a bungalow on the left and Deadman's Lane ahead. Cross the lane into the fenced path opposite and, over a stile, bear left to follow the field edge with the fence on the left to a well-defined path on the right. Then it's straight across the middle of the field to a small gate against the opposite hedge. Turn left through the gate and walk to a stile to go over it and down the path ahead toward a group of buildings: Goring Heath Primary School was one of those on the right. Turn left across the courtyard of Alnutt's Hospital, a group of ten almshouses surrounding a chapel complete with splendid white clock tower. In his will, in 1724, Henry Alnutt left money for the almshouses and the chapel in the charming courtyard and overlooking wide open views of the Berkshire countryside. By the sign 'Chaplaincy' follow the grassy path on the right for a short distance to a gate onto the crossroads at Goring Heath.

Go to the right of the post office which, incidentally, serves cold drinks, light lunches and teas with home-made cakes as well as all manner of other needs including stamps. There you will find a path through trees which leads to a path on the right at a field edge. Turn right onto this path for a few yards with a high hedge on the left and a wire fence on the right and then, having crossed a stile, plunge diagonally across a grass field to reach a stile on the other side onto Bunce's Lane. Cross the lane to walk between the cottages opposite, through a metal gate and over a stile on the right. Here follow the path alongside the woodland on the left and on down and uphill over stiles through the broad sweeping valley of Path Hill and up onto the hill itself through a narrow brake of woodland. Turn left onto the lane and walk past Path Hill Farm and, about 120 or so yards into the wood on the far side, in a hollow of a dell, turn left down another woodland track.

At the bottom of the valley, opposite a field exit on the left, turn right and then fork left onto a well-defined path climbing gently uphill to the wood edge. Here do not take the stile ahead toward a white cottage but instead turn left over another stile and up the edge of the field with the hedge on the right to a small wooden gate onto the road at Collins End Common.

Turn left along the road and, about 80 yards after 'Briar Cottage' on the right, turn right along a fenced track and when this bends right, go ahead over a ramshackle stile into the field ahead. Continue over the fields and two more stiles to cross a small paddock to a stile opposite with the King Charles Head on the far side of the road.

Chazey Heath
The Packhorse

Chazey Heath, which derives its name from the manor of Mapledurham Chawsey, or Chausey as it was known in the Middle Ages, is a hilltop settlement now part of the parish of Mapledurham and lies on the ancient 'pack and prime' route through Henley and Reading to Wallingford. Within its bounds is a 13th to 15th century farmhouse known as Chazey Court, which is of some historic and architectural interest, but more important is Mapledurham Manor House, the focus of this walk. There is only a steep narrow lane into Mapledurham from the A4074 at Chazey Heath so that it remains relatively undisturbed by modern traffic and busy-ness.

The Packhorse, at Chazey Heath, a squat, low-ceilinged 400 year old inn, is very much a family pub. The long lounge bar is simply furnished, with a huge log fire burning in its grate on colder days, and there is an adjoining family room. A large garden is at the back, bordered by woods and with tables and benches and playthings for the children. Well-kept Gale's real ales are served: HSB, BBB, and Best Bitter. Gale's traditional country wines, of which there are 21, are also

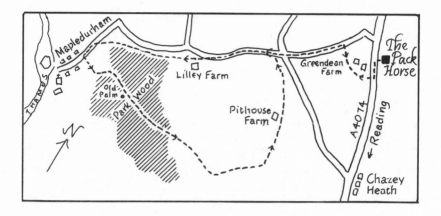

featured. They are listed according to their sweetness or dryness: for example, birch and damson are dry, while apricot, raspberry and black beer and raisin are sweet. Natural grape juice is used to initiate fermentation but the basis of all the wines is the natural fruit, berry or seed and interesting and delicious flavours are achieved from them. Opening times are from 11 am to 3 pm and from 7 pm to 11 pm except Sundays when the inn closes at 10.30 pm. Meals are served at lunchtime and in the evening (except on Sunday evenings). These include special home-made pâtés, also Cornish smoked mackerel and a vegetarian moussaka.

Telephone: 0734 722140.

How to get there: Chazey Heath lies high above the river on the A4074 Reading to Woodcote road. The Packhorse is on the right hand side of the road at the far end of the village.

Parking: There is ample parking in front of the inn. Do let the staff know if you intend to leave the car while you walk.

Length of the walk: 5 miles. Map: OS Pathfinder 1172 (GR 692781).

Magnificent views of rolling, hilly countryside reward some steep climbs on this walk to the tiny, unhurried hamlet of Mapledurham, lying alongside a broad stretch of the river below wooded slopes and heathland. Allow time to explore the church and the manor house and mill (if they are open) and to revel in the antiquity and peace.

The Walk

Turn left out of the pub and walk down the road past Greendean Farm to take a path on the right just past it through the farmyard and turn left again onto a lane at a thatched cottage. Go straight across the crossroads as for Mapledurham House and mill. Go on past Lilley Farm and, just past the last of the farm buildings, take the path on the left into a field and walk down parallel with the road toward Park Wood, which seems, by the noise, to be teeming with pheasants. Go over a stile directly ahead and go straight across a second field by an obvious path; below to the right in the valley is the beautiful warm, red-brick farmhouse of Bottom Farm. Breasting the little hill, marvellous curves of the river appear ahead. Walk on across the field to a stile in the left hand corner onto the lane into Mapledurham village. Beside the mill, on the right, is a track leading to the lock and the river bank.

Return up the lane, having explored the village, and turn right into the bridleway, The Warren, and, after a few yards, take a marked path over a stile on the left. Cross the field towards the wood and cross another stile on the far side and straight ahead to yet another stile. From here follow the well-trodden path steeply uphill and along the contours of the hill. The views to the right, of parkland, flat meadows and sleepily rolling river are spectacular. At the top of the hill is Old Palm, a huge stone statue of a man on a brick pedestal looking out over the riparian scene and bearing a pitcher under his arm. No-one knows who he is or why he is there, he's just Old Palm! Turn right onto a broader track at a T junction and follow the path through woodland carpeted with white wild wood anemones in early spring and, later on, with bluebells. Cross a broad track in open country and go straight ahead towards Rose Farm. Turn left as the path bears round between the house and the farm buildings and then straight ahead along a grassy track on the high, hilltop plateau with the land dropping steeply away to the right towards Reading. Go over a stile and forge straight ahead, ignoring all side turnings, to a stile in the corner of a hedge on the right. Go over the stile and follow the path leftward and downhill making for Pithouse Farm and a white cottage; the path passes between the two. Emerge onto the farm track and follow it to the left for about ⅓ mile past a flourishing pig farm. Turn right at the end of the farm track onto the lane and cross the road after a few yards to continue on the original lane, turning right off it beside the thatched cottage. Follow the path back to the A4074 and turn left to find the pub facing the road on the right.

Rotherfield Greys
The Maltster's Arms

Set on the southern slopes of the Chilterns, above the great loop of
the Thames between Henley and Reading, this tiny village holds the
very essence of rural England. Greys is famous for its superbly
blossoming cherry orchards and for Greys Court, a Tudor house and
garden set in the ruins of an earlier, 14th century, fortress.

The Maltster's Arms is 250 years old but it has not always been a pub
having once been the coach-house to a local great house. There is
reputed to be a ghost, not seen lately, a maiden aunt who comes back
to visit the bedroom in which she died. The white-painted building
stands squarely on a bend in the road next door to the delightful old
Saxon church. Beyond the car park is a pleasant grassy garden set with
tables and benches and with a panoramic view at all times of the year.
Entering the porch one is immediately charmed by the sight of an
ancient oak settle, highly polished, and set against the wall. Through
the thick, blackened doorway are three bars, joined in an E-shape. The
decor is charming and restful, soft grey/pink cushioned banquettes
and chairs, small tables and a proper fire burning brightly on the far

side on colder days. Pleasant prints of gun dogs adorn the walls and the whole atmosphere is one of quiet friendliness. Well-behaved children are welcomed for meals (there's a children's menu).

As a Brakspear's house, all the brewery's real ales are sold, as are six wines – two red and four white, ranging from very sweet to a dry – by the glass. The menu is extensive; the day's 'specials', such as soup of the day, mushrooms on toast, mussels in garlic, cottage pie and corned beef hash, followed by a seductively delicious selection of home-made sweets, are listed on blackboards above the fireplace. Home-baked crusty French bread and rolls are used for the ploughman's lunches and for 'crusty rollers' with fillings and salad garnish. The standard, printed menu includes home-made lamb Madras, hot chicken and ham pie, fisherman's pie and several vegetarian dishes.

Opening times are from 11.30 am to 2.30 pm and from 5.30 pm to 11 pm except on Sundays when they are from noon to 3 pm and from 7 pm to 10.30 pm. Bar meals are served at lunchtimes and in the evening every day.

Telephone: 04917 400.

How to get there: Rotherfield Greys is on an unclassified road 2½ miles west of Henley. From the war memorial follow the lane signposted to Greys church.

Parking: A good-sized car park lies between the church and the pub.

Length of the walk: 3 miles. Map: OS Pathfinder 1156 (GR 726824).

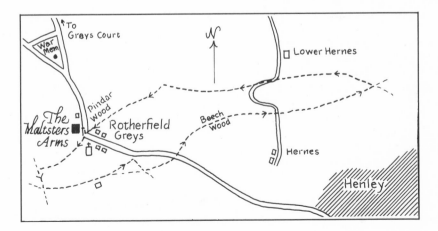

There are exceptional views from many points on this countryside walk, which also takes you through fine beech woods.

The Walk

Turn right out of the pub towards the church and take the path on the right between them. Go over a stile and straight across the field ahead with magnificent distant views all around. Go over the next stile and bear slightly to the right over the field to another stile. Go over it and turn left onto the track below, following it for a few yards to a gate. Go through the gate and take the metalled track on the extreme left following it for about ½ mile past a pleasant house on the right and on to a T junction to take the marked path immediately on the right and cross the field to a stile about halfway up the fence on the left hand side. Cross the lane here to a track opposite marked 'Bridleway – Henley 2' and follow this lovely walk through a beautiful strip of beechwood with glimpses steeply downhill through the trees to the deep valley below, with a thriving and noisy pig farm in between.

The track crosses a private drive to Hernes and continues out into open country with wide views of rolling countryside to left and right and meanders gently downhill. At a cross-track at the foot of the valley go over the stile on the left to follow the track back along the valley keeping to the lower path with the fence on the left. Soon the lovely red-brick and timbered farmhouse of Lower Hernes can be seen ahead backed by a densely wooded thicket. Walk past the farm and on along the valley floor following the track ahead. Where it veers sharply left, go over a stile on the right and follow the path close to the hedge on the left. About 10 yards after crossing the next stile, take the path over a stile on the left and follow it along the field edge to another one. Cross this stile and turn left to climb steeply uphill following the contours of the field past the corner of Pindar Wood. More pigs are guffling noisily from their water troughs on the left. Follow the path as it flattens out to cross the field at the hilltop to emerge onto the road opposite the little church and The Maltster's Arms.

To view the house and gardens of the National Trust's Greys Court, open to the public on certain days (not Sundays) from Easter to October, bear right at the war memorial and the entrance to the house is on the left down the steep lane.

Sonning
The Bull Inn

During the 10th and 11th centuries Sonning was one of the largest parishes in Wessex and boasted three successive Archbishops of Canterbury. Sonning was a well-known place when nearby Reading was only a handful of huts beside the river Kennet but Reading's importance grew as Sonning's waned. Today it is a beautiful and peaceful village of warm red-brick and timbered cottages and houses, narrow streets and a lovely old church, St. Andrew's, set on the tranquil bank of the river Thames. Its peace often used to be disturbed, it is said, by the arrival of Dick Turpin the highwayman at his aunt's cottage by the churchyard after a raid somewhere along the Bath road nearby. There was an underground stable below the cottage and Black Bess would make her way into this while her master raced through the churchyard and across the river bridge to the Oxfordshire side where he could lie up quietly till the hue and cry was over.

The Bull is set in its own quiet courtyard at the end of the narrow road leading to the church. Once frequently used by pilgrims travelling to and from London and Canterbury, it dates from the 14th century and the timbered ceilings and deep fireplaces are original. In

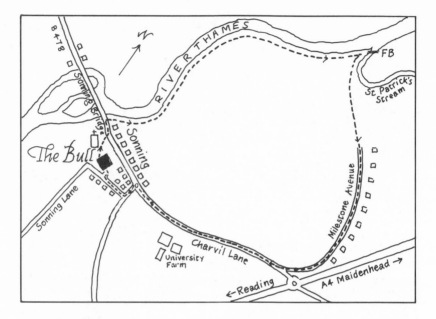

1574 the land on which the inn stands passed from the ownership of the church to that of the crown; the entrance to the churchyard forms a part of The Bull's yard.

The inn boasts an impressive collection of prizes for its Wethered ales, won through six consecutive years. Wine is sold by the glass, a very palatable red and two varieties of white, a dry and a sweeter wine. The restaurant is open every evening, Sundays and Mondays excepted, from 7.30 pm to 9.30 pm. At lunchtime there is an attractive cold table set at the back of the bar from which one helps oneself to a great variety of salads with game pie, smoked mackerel, ham and chicken or turkey accompanied by crisply fresh rolls. The inn is open from 12 noon to 2 pm and from 5.30 pm to 11 pm Monday to Saturday, and from 12 noon to 2 pm and 7 pm to 10.30 pm on Sundays. There are benches and tables all round the attractive yard, gloriously bedecked with hanging baskets for much of the year. The compact bar is warmly welcoming when the fires are alight.

Telephone: 0734 693901.

How to get there: Sonning is about 1 mile off the A4 east of Reading. There are three lanes to the village, so plenty of chances to find it. The Bull is at the end of a cul-de-sac leading to the church, to the left off the short High Street.

Parking: There is parking in front of the inn courtyard or in the lane.

Length of the walk: 3 miles. Map: OS Pathfinder 1172 (GR 755756).

A pleasant stroll beside the Thames north of Sonning for a mile or so, full of interest with countless river craft in summer, still and atmospheric in winter, and back to this attractive village along tracks and lanes.

The Walk
From the yard of The Bull go through the kissing gate to walk through the churchyard and turn left into the road at the other end. Take the towpath on the right just before the traffic lights at the bridge and follow it alongside the river for a good mile. The bank is high on this side as are the willows from time to time obscuring the view of the water. Meadowsweet, scabious and ragwort can make grand splashes of colour along the path's side. In summer the river is busy with craft of all shapes and sizes and colours but in the winter the water is grey and quiet and the hills in the distance are blue tinged above the water-meadows on the left bank. The path emerges onto a gravel track alongside a high wooden fence by a footbridge. Turn right away from the bridge and follow the track on as it becomes a metalled road between the flat fields of Reading University farm on the right and meadowland, a riot of colour in the summer, with toadflax, ragwort, meadowsweet and willow herb all rampaging away vigorously. In about a quarter of a mile small houses, set back behind well-kept gardens are to be seen on the left.

Follow the road, Milestone Avenue, to its end almost against the Bath road and turn right down Charvil Lane to walk back to Sonning village past the University farm buildings and some delightful old houses and cottages. Walk straight across the little roundabout and turn left just past a large, pink-painted house on the left hand side of the road. Follow the lane down alongside a high flint wall and turn right again at Mr. Palmer's water pump on the corner to return to The Bull and the car.

Shiplake Row
The White Hart

This 17th century inn, now an imposing, tall white building, at one time occupied only half the premises it presently uses; the other half was a butcher's shop and they were both thatched. The butcher's shop was eventually renovated and joined in with the inn and both were then slated rather than thatched. There is a huge log fire burning just inside the door in winter, a horseshoe shaped bar and a restaurant area beyond this. The inn is pleasantly but plainly furnished and has a large, grassy garden at the rear which is in constant use during the summer. The local countryside is honeycombed with footpaths and is outstandingly attractive. The White Hart is a great rendezvous for walkers and ramblers surge into the bar in great numbers and stockinged feet for well-earned refreshment.

The enormous menu appears on three blackboards above the bar. On Sundays there is a lunch of roast meat and five vegetables in season and plenty of home-made hot dishes of meats and fish, as well as some vegetarian meals, appear on other days. Brakspear real ales are on sale and there's a large selection of wines in addition to the three house wines which are sold by the glass. Table d'hôte lunch is served every day; on Sunday it is à la carte.

The inn is open from 12 noon until 2.30 pm and from 7.30 pm to 11 pm all week.

Telephone: 0734 403673.

How to get there: The hamlet of Shiplake Row lies about ½ mile from Shiplake proper. Leave the A4155 Henley to Reading road by a turning on the right (Memorial Avenue) about ¼ mile from a crossroads with a war memorial. At the T junction at the end of the avenue turn right and The White Hart inn is another ¼ mile up the lane on the left.

Parking: The car park is small for the size and popularity of the pub, so you can find space in the lane opposite if necessary.

Length of the walk: 4 miles. Map: OS Pathfinder 1172 (GR 756787).

A varied walk of woodland, followed by large houses and glorious gardens and about a mile of river bank, passing Shiplake church with its ancient stained glass.

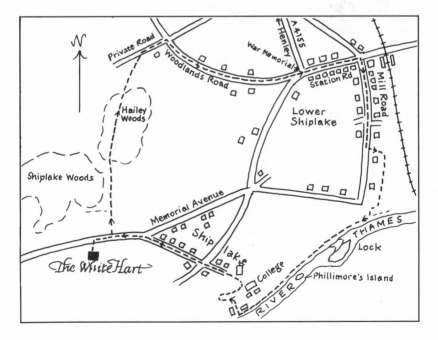

The Walk

Turn right out of the pub and follow the lane for about 200 yards to take a track on the left. There are excellent views of the distant wooded hills above Wargrave from here. After another 100 yards, take a right fork onto a path to follow it down and uphill through Lower and Upper Hailey Woods, a large area of mixed woodland. Continue out of the wood and straight ahead on the path across a wide field and, on the far side, turn right into a quiet private road. Follow this for 100 yards or so to Woodlands Road and turn right again. Huge and well-kept properties, set back in shrubby gardens, lie on the left. Soon, on the right, is a stables and its majestic iron gateway has three square pillars topped by three very realistically sculpted eagles. Cross the major road at the end of Woodland Road and continue ahead down Station Road for about ½ mile crossing to walk on the footway on the left hand side. Large pre-war houses set back in comfortable and spacious gardens on the left contrast with the smaller, modern houses on the right. At the Baskerville Arms turn right into Mill Road towards Lower Shiplake and Lashbrook and follow this road for nearly a mile.

After this the road is intersected by paths on either side; take the path on the left behind a pillar box and after about 40 yards, on the far side of a bridge over the lake, turn right over a stile into a field and left over another stile to follow the field path with the fence on the right. After two more stiles turn right and then almost immediately left onto a path to the river bank; turn right to walk along the river for a mile or so. The land rises steeply from the river on the right and, on the hilltop, is the very grand white mansion, Shiplake House and, a little further along, the red-brick rambling Victorian buildings of Shiplake College. In the middle of the river is the tiny Phillimore's Island covered in trees. By the college boathouses and just before the small footbridge on the towpath, turn right to take a path between the boathouses and alongside one with big green doors. After about 150 yards, at a crosstrack, take a tiny hairpin path on the right into woodland and follow it steeply uphill behind the college to emerge at the little flint church of St. Peter and St. Paul, Shiplake.

Turn left to walk past the church along the lane to a crossroads with The Plowden Arms on the opposite corner. Cross the road to the lane signposted for Binfield Heath and follow it, past houses on the right and wide views of farmland on the left, past the school and the exit of Memorial Avenue on the right. After another ¼ mile The White Hart is reached on the left of the lane.

Henley-on-Thames
The Angel

The narrow passages and doorways, the profusion of oak beams and the uneven and creaky floors of The Angel tell of its early 17th century origins. In the cellar is a stone and flint arch which purports to be part of the original mediaeval bridge over the river. Certainly history relates that an inn has stood on this site since the 14th century at least. If walls could speak what secrets would The Angel's walls have to tell? It has had its part in history through the ages having been fought over and around during the Civil War and, in a door in the lounge, is a fragment of stained glass dated 1250 from the Chapter House of Westminster Abbey which was shattered by a bomb in 1940.

Stone steps lead from the street level at the side of the inn to what used to be a busy landing stage and is now the equally busy Terrace Bar. There is a quiet and well-furnished bar in the pub itself overlooking the bustling river scene and the bridge crossing it. The restaurant serves luncheons and dinners daily and there is an enormously comprehensive menu of hot and cold bar meals to be had. There are twelve hot dishes, highly recommended, among them

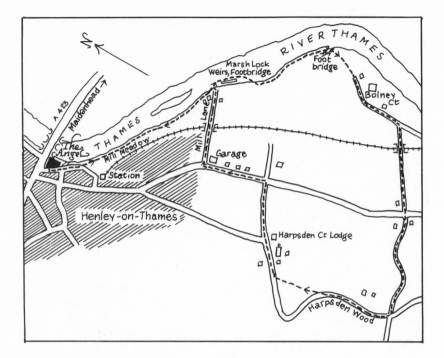

being the guinea fowl braised in Madeira with a garnish of fresh vegetables. Jacket potatoes with various fillings, four different cheese or pâté ploughman's and a wide choice of sandwiches and salads are offered. The Terrace Bar has a very slightly less wide menu but, on a hot and sunny day, what could be more delightful than to sit beside this lively little bit of river to be served by cheerful young people and surrounded by pleasant company? Brakspear ales are served, as is wine by the glass. There is a full list of wines to buy by the bottle.

Opening times are weekdays 11 am to 11 pm and on Sundays, 12 pm to 3 pm and 7 pm to 10.30 pm.

Telephone: 0492 410678.

How to get there: From the A423 (Maidenhead/Henley road) the inn is immediately on the left, just over the river bridge, fronting Angel Street and backed by the river.

Parking: Park in a public car park. The one at Mill Meadow is reached by turning left from Angel Street after about ½ mile. Return to The Angel on foot for refreshment and the walk.

Length of the walk: 4 miles. Map: OS Pathfinder 1156 (GR 763825).

About 1½ miles along the trim towpath to pass the attractive weirs at Marsh Lock, with plenty of interest on the river as you go. Back by way of Harpsden Wood and mostly quiet lanes to rejoin the river for views of Henley the other way round.

The Walk

Turn left out of The Angel and follow the river bank as nearly as possible past charming old Tudor and Georgian houses and on to the grassy towing path. Well-kept lawns and wooden seats are found all along on the right bank while densely tree-clad hills rise steeply from the other, Wargrave, side of the river. Soon, on a long narrow island in the middle of the river, is a veritable estate of small holiday bungalows.

Marsh Lock is reached over a series of bridges and the towpath is rejoined beyond them. On the opposite bank are large, prestigious Edwardian mansions in meticulously manicured lawns and gardens. After about ½ mile the path veers to the right leaving the river bank and crosses a small footbridge to continue past a house on the left and beside its drive, alongside which runs the track of a miniature railway. Walk along the road at the end of the path, past more very large properties, to a fork and bear right to go over the railway line and on down the lane, a tree-lined avenue, to a major road. Cross the road to follow the track opposite to a crossroads, turn right into a quiet lane which meanders gently downhill through Harpsden Wood. After ½ mile strike off onto a marked path on the right down through the wood to cut off a large bulge in the lane. Turn right onto the lane for Henley and, just after the tiny church, take a narrow lane on the right past Harpsden Court Lodge and follow it for 300 yards to another major road. Turn left onto it for 400 yards of no path and busy traffic – it doesn't last long! Turn right just past the Burmah garage into Mill Lane and follow it back to Marsh Lock. Turn left here to follow the towpath and then to cross the grass to the car park.

Bix
The Fox Inn

Bix is an unremarkable little collection of houses and cottages on the A423 and has no shop or post office. Its greatest claim to fame is that it lies beside only the second strip of dual carriageway to be laid in this country, the first being the Winchester bypass. In fact, the original Fox Inn, a small brick and flint alehouse, lay exactly in the middle of the proposed route of the carriageway so it was demolished and, in 1935, the present Fox Inn was built. The building is very typical 1930s, between-the-wars architecture but its lines are softened by an exuberant virginia creeper which clambers and romps about it, brilliantly colourful in late summer and autumn. Beside and behind the house is a good-sized garden with tables and benches and a hitching rail for horses, frequently used. There is uncluttered space for children, who are not allowed in the bars, to play. But what makes this pub so special is the very welcoming and friendly atmosphere. There are two bars: an attractively wood-panelled lounge with a huge log fire in winter, and gleaming copperware hung round the chimney for decoration and a small, 'farmer's', bar which can also have a log fire. The rooms are spotless, the 'offices' immaculate and there is plenty of table space for eating. Down the long front-facing wall are a series of amusing 'foxy' pictures and prints and the shorter wall has a splendid window with a deep sill to hold flowering plants.

The food is all home-made and freshly cooked and the menu features pizzas, lasagne, steak and kidney pie and some very tasty game dishes which are served during the winter. The Fox is a Brakspear's house so the brewery's own real ales are sold; in winter Bitter and Old Ale and in summer the Old Ale is replaced with Special. Three wines, two white and a red, are available by the glass. Opening hours are from 11 am to 3 pm and from 7 pm to 11 pm. Meals are served both at lunchtime and in the evening.

Telephone: 0491 574143.

How to get there: The Fox Inn is on the right of the A423 about 2 miles north west of Henley.

Parking: Park in the ample car park.

Length of the walk: 4 miles. Map: OS Pathfinder 1156 (GR 725853).

This is a walk of peaceful beech woods and extensive views, beautiful at any time of year, but especially in the spring when bluebells fill the woods and green shoots cover the curving slopes of the fields. An entirely rural route; strong footwear is advisable.

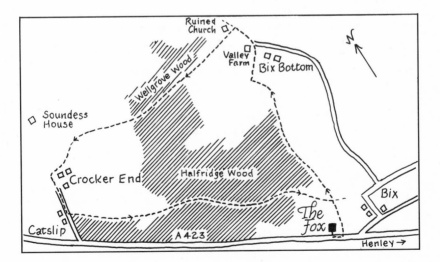

The Walk

Turn left out of the pub and left again after a few yards, over a broken stile into a large field. Cross the field by the clearly marked path, over a bridletrack, to a stile into the woods opposite. Cross the stile and follow the clear path on the left for about 150 yards and then bear a little right to follow the path gently downhill to the wood edge. Bluebells carpet the floor of this ancient beech wood in the late spring and there are magnificent views of rolling countryside to the right. Bear right again soon onto a broader track near the edge of the wood. At its end turn left to cross a stile above Valley Farm and walk steeply downhill to another stile where turn right toward the farm buildings.

Through the farmyard turn left onto a lane and, at the ruins of the small Saxon flint church of St. James, turn left again onto a marked path to walk steadily uphill toward Wellgrove Wood. There are wide views all around; only, perhaps, the squawk of a pheasant to disturb the peace. Follow the track through the wood as straight ahead as possible and ignoring all side turnings. You will notice the prevalence of dark-green leaved Dog's Mercury carpeting the wood; this is a sign of ancient woodland as it takes the plant hundreds of years to become established and flourish. At the end of the wood go over an awkwardly high stile and cross the field ahead with a good view of Soundess House to the right. Keep the hedge on the left and emerge at Crocker End over a stile and along a drive. Just past Bee's Cottage turn left into a lane and follow it past some charming cottages and The Carpenter's Arms and then gently down and uphill to Catslip. Here take the gravel track on the left past a white cottage and follow it straight ahead as it becomes a grassy track into Halfridge Wood. Keep straight on, ignoring all side turnings and finally crossing a broad track at the wood edge to follow the path downhill into open country again. About three quarters of the way across the field ahead turn right onto the original path opposite the corner of a copper beech hedge and follow it back to the road, turning right to find The Fox.

Fawley
The Walnut Tree

Fawley village is isolated on a north to south ridge of hills above the Thames and is approached by narrow, winding, tree-lined lanes. The Walnut Tree is an incongruous, rather ugly, building amid the 17th to 18th century brick and timber cottages of the village. It was built in 1957 and took some time to complete as all the cellars are hand-dug. Apparently the builder or the brewery hedged their bets: if it proved impossible to obtain a licence in so isolated a place, it could serve as a dwelling house just as well! Fortunately it did get its licence and has provided sustenance for the local community and visitors, from far and wide, ever since.

This Brakspear's house has always had a reputation for good food, along with its well-kept real ales, friendly and welcoming atmosphere and pleasant and efficient service. At the side of the inn there is a large lawn set with tables and benches and in front, a terrace also has garden furniture and can be a delightful sun-trap on a fine day. The interior is pleasantly and simply furnished and a log fire burns there on cold winter days. There is an attractive conservatory-type restaurant where

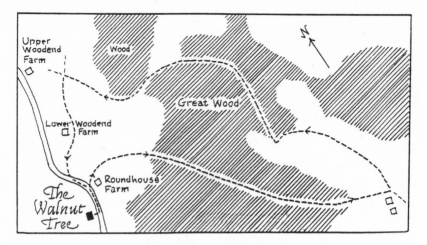

children are made welcome. Food is served both at lunchtime and in the evenings, and afternoon teas are served in the garden during the summer. The menu, which is no 'run-of-the-mill sausages and chips' type of thing, appears on a blackboard at the side of the bar and some of the dishes are changed daily but the popular ones, like mushrooms cooked with a thick white wine and cheese sauce or a half-pint tankard of huge prawns served with a dip and salad, are constants. Unusual main course meals can be breast of duck with honey and thyme, vegetarian rosti and liver with mushroom and asparagus. There are speciality ices to follow. As well as bitters of the brewery, there is a wide selection of wines from the local Fawley vineyard and a good selection of malt whiskies. Six house wines are sold by the glass.

Opening hours are from 11 am to 3 pm and from 6 pm to 11 pm; in winter the pub closes at 2.30 in the afternoon.

Telephone: 0491 163360.

How to get there: Fawley, north of Henley, can be reached by lanes off the A4155 Henley to Marlow road. The Walnut Tree is on the left at the far end of the village.

Parking: Park at the front of the pub.

Length of the walk: 3½ miles. Map: OS Pathfinder 1156 (GR 758873).

A most peaceful ramble over farmland and through woodland with, quite possibly, only the squirrels for company. Far-reaching views to the hills beyond and glimpses of the Thames in the valley below.

94

The Walk

Turn left out of the pub and follow the lane for about 150 yards to a sharp left bend in the road, then take the marked track on the right just past Round House Farm and alongside the Round House itself. On the right are magnificent views to the hills of Oxfordshire in the far distance. Go straight ahead on the track past a white house and into Great Wood, where there is a profusion of wild cherry blossom in the early spring and bluebells carpet the woodland floor. As nearly as possible follow the well-defined and arrowed track straight ahead going gently and then quite steeply downhill through the wood and out into open country. Here there are splendid views of the river below, through the trees, as it meanders, to left and right, past Hambleden and towards Henley. On the left across the valley a hillside, devastated by the storms of 1990, has been replanted with sturdy young trees; the hill curves majestically ahead, backed by woodland of beech and wild cherry.

At the T junction at the foot of the valley, turn left to follow the track along the valley floor. Cross an intersection and go straight ahead on the broad path, with a bank of violets on the left and a leafy valley below it. Pheasants squawk and hurry about all over the place. Enter the wood again at a path junction and bear left onto a narrower bridletrack, going more steeply uphill through the wood and emerging finally into wide, open farmland. Just before reaching the large red-brick house and buildings of Upper Woodend Farm, go over a stile on the left into a field and cross towards the buildings of Lower Woodend. Here there are wonderful open views again far and wide across the countryside. Go over another stile in the fence opposite about ⅔ of the way down. Go through a gate ahead and follow the path and then a drive walking past the farm buildings and onto the lane. Here turn left to return to The Walnut Tree along the road past Round House Farm again on the left.

Aston
The Flower Pot

This delightful Victorian inn – calling itself The Flower Pot Hotel and catering for 'boating parties and fishermen' – takes one at once back to Jerome K. Jerome's 'Three Men in a Boat' era. It is located almost at the end of a narrow, leafy lane running past colourful gardens to the river Thames and has its own landing stage ½ mile from Hambleden Lock and 2 miles along the river from Henley. Built around 1890 to replace an earlier inn of the same name, The Flower Pot has now been refurbished to provide all modern facilities but it still retains its lovely Victorian character. It has a large open garden at the back of the hotel from which there are magnificent views of the densely tree-clad hills on the far bank of the river and smiling meadows in the foreground. The landlord drives a pre-1925 Rolls Royce in black and yellow which stands importantly in the car park when not in use, lending a gentler, less hurried air to the surroundings.

Enquiries elicit the information that it's easier to tell people when the inn is closed rather than when it is open; it is closed from 3.30 pm to 5.30 pm every day. Otherwise it is open to serve all meals from breakfast onward. Evening meals are not served on Sunday or Monday but there is an attractive menu of bar lunches, hot and cold, every day. Sandwiches are prepared individually and delicious crusty French bread is served with a variety of fillings including superb cold beef and salad. The inn glories in its real ales, which are Brakspear XXX Mild in summer and Bitter, Special and Old Ale in winter. Wine is served by the glass and there is a small, but good, range of wines to buy by the bottle.

Opening hours are from 8.30 am to 11 pm and after for house guests.

Telephone: 0491 574721.

How to get there: Aston is signposted from the A423, 2 miles from Henley on the left or 5½ miles from the large roundabout past Maidenhead Thicket on the right. The inn lies about 1 mile down the lane on the left.

Parking: Park at the inn.

Length of the walk: 3½ miles. Map: OS Pathfinder 1156 (GR 785842).

A delightful, largely riverside, walk passing Temple Island, the furthest point of the rowing races at Henley Regatta. The route back by way of Remenham church, offers superb open views.

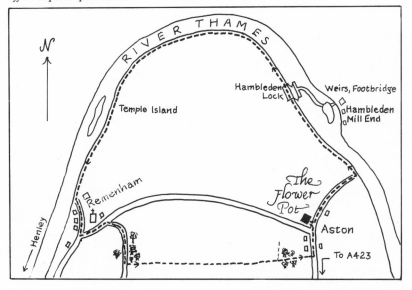

The Walk

Turn left past the side of the inn to follow the same lane for 200 yards to the river bank and then turn left along the towing path, bright in summer with the purple flower of willowherb. In ½ mile Hambleden Lock is reached. On the opposite bank are the old mill buildings, now the home of a prestigious sailing club. There are four weirs which can be crossed by bridges if desired but the walk proceeds over the lock and on again along the towpath with the squat tower of the parish church of St. Mary the Virgin at Henley ahead in the distance. There are two or three pleasant houses on the opposite bank, and, very soon the white Palladian mansion and buildings of the Management College come into view over immaculate lawns and beside shady old cedar trees. After about a mile Temple Island is reached; it does have a cupola'd temple tucked among its trees. After another ⅓ mile the towpath forks just past River House; take the left fork here and go over the stile alongside the wall of the house to follow the track to Remenham church. Walk past the pretty and peaceful looking church and turn left at the T junction. After a few yards take a right fork, signposted Maidenhead, and follow the lane gently uphill through the trees. At the end of the wood turn left onto a marked footpath by a large metal gate. Here there are marvellous open views to left and right. After about ¾ of a mile cross a track coming uphill on the left to a rather overgrown footpath opposite and follow this downhill over a field to emerge onto the lane at Aston just a few yards from The Flower Pot. Turn left to find it and the parked car.

Medmenham
The Dog and Badger

This attractive 16th century inn, with its ancient timbered bar, has seen a lot of interesting goings-on over the years. Nell Gwyn is reputed to have met some of her admirers here, Thames Swan-uppers held 'great dinners' in its dining room and Sir Francis Dashwood, the noted Satanist, and his cronies from the Hell-fire Club, which met in Medmenham Abbey, came to drink at the bar. Until 1899 the Parish Clerk of Medmenham read the banns of marriage in the inn before they were published in the church.

The inn is open every day at lunchtime and in the evening. (Weekdays, 11.30 am to 3 pm, 6 pm to 11 pm. Sundays, 12 noon to 3 pm, 7 pm to 10.30 pm.) Sunday lunch in the restaurant is a speciality with all of five appetisers and six main courses as a rule; the set table d'hôte menu changes each week and there is an à la carte menu. In addition a good selection of daily 'specials' is displayed on a blackboard in the bar. Sandwiches are generous and there is a choice of brown or white bread. Among the hot dishes there is sometimes a deliciously home-cooked and cheesy lasagne with plenty of meat and

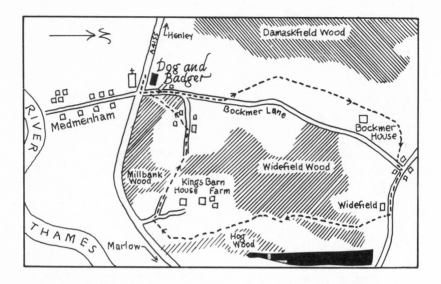

served with 'proper' chips. Five house wines are sold by the glass and there is a comprehensive wine list. Of ales there are many: Ruddles, Wethered Bitter, Flowers Original, Brakspear's and Wadworth 6X.

Telephone: 0491 571362.

How to get there: The Dog and Badger lies on the A4155 road from Marlow to Henley, just beyond the brow of the hill near Medmenham Abbey. It is on the right hand corner of a crossroads, the lane on the left leading past the church into Medmenham village itself.

Parking: There is ample parking space, carved out of the chalky hillside, by the inn.

Length of the walk: 3 miles. Map: OS Pathfinder 1157 (GR 806845).

Enjoy this ramble through fields and woods just north of the Thames and later take time, if you can, to explore the village of Medmenham, the last true riverside village in Bucks, and its historic church.

The Walk
Turn left out of the pub and walk up the narrow lane on the far side of it, Bockmer Lane, past pleasant, comfortable cottages and high, dense woodland on the right. Keep to the left at the fork in the lane

and walk gently uphill through mixed woodland and take a stile on the left by a large wooden gate very shortly. Follow the marked path slightly diagonally across the first field, then straight across the next ones, bearing right on the path beyond Bockmer House to emerge onto the lane and turn left here to walk a few yards to a T junction. There are sometimes lively horses in the second field so you may prefer to keep to the lane with its wide views of open pastureland backed by dense woodland. Turn right at the T junction by a little triangle of grass.

Follow this road past a large establishment called Widefield on the right and, in a very few yards, take the marked footpath, well concealed in the hedge on the right, and turn left over a stile into a field. Cross this field to a stile on the far side and turn right onto a track on the other side. After 10 yards or so go over a stile on the left into a wood. Follow the well-defined path, bordered at first by laurel and beech, and then up a short, steep bank and out into open country again where the path weaves drunkenly between the stumps of fallen trees. Carry on walking along the path parallel with the wood edge with a steep valley falling away on the left. Go over a stile on the right and follow the path across the valley floor to a stile opposite. Cross a track to another stile and follow the path bearing right and, after 10 yards, turn left uphill into another wood. The path follows the wood edge with Kings Barn Farm and Kings Barn House deep in the valley on the right.

Some 200 yards past the farm buildings there is a tiny footpath on the right going steeply downhill to a driveway. Take this path, turn right onto the drive and left at the fork signposted 'Pheasantry'. Here there are superb views especially to the right. Follow the path uphill and cross a triangle of grass beyond the wood onto a metalled track and follow this to the Old School. Here take the path on the left, crossing a drive and follow it opposite as it curves downhill through the wood to emerge on the corner of Bockmer Lane. Turn right onto the main road to return to The Dog and Badger. In very wet or muddy conditions, it may be easier to follow the lane past the Old School and on downhill to join the original lane at the fork and go on to the main road and turn right.

Hurley
The Olde Bell

The village of Hurley lies halfway exactly between Oxford and London. It has been a settlement since the Bronze Age and there are some interesting houses in the village: Hurley House, in the High Street, is 17th century and nearby are three charming almshouses of the same date. Hurley Priory, situated by the river, was founded by Geoffrey de Mandeville in 1056 for monks from Westminster Abbey. It was, of course, dissolved by Henry VIII but vestiges of a stone cloister and monks' dormitories near the church can still be seen. The large tithe barn, now a private dwelling, and the dovecote date from the mid-13th century and give an indication of the one-time wealth and influence of the priory in the locality.

The Olde Bell, built to serve as the guest house of the priory, is the oldest coaching inn in England and dates from 1135. Its old and picturesque exterior belies the luxury of the appointments within. The large, elegant bar is well stocked with single malt whiskies, popular brands of gin and vodka, a variety of brandies and some less often seen liqueurs, all of which are backed up by a huge and selective wine list.

Very good house wine is served by the glass, and beers include Worthington and Tennent's. This inn has an undeniable reputation for excellence so its bar meals are not cheap; smoked salmon, smoked chicken and terrine of duck are served imaginatively with attractive salad additions and there is a large choice of sandwiches. The restaurant is open for lunch and dinner each day and there is a huge menu from which to choose. An example of a main course dish is supreme of chicken with mango and coconut in a curry cream. Outside is a pleasantly furnished garden with a tiny fountain backed by shrubs and trees in differing shades of green.

The inn is open from 11 am to 2.30 pm and 6 pm to 11 pm weekdays and on Sundays, 12 pm to 3 pm and 7 pm to 10.30 pm.

Telephone: 0628 825881.

How to get there: Hurley is reached on a lane signposted from the A423 Maidenhead to Henley road, about 1½ miles from the large roundabout beyond Maidenhead Thicket.

Parking: There is a spacious car park opposite The Olde Bell.

Length of the walk: 5 miles. Map: OS Pathfinder 1157 (GR 827835).

This interesting walk includes Hurley Lock and more than 2 miles of towpath. Combine it with a stroll around the village, taking in the 17th century almshouses and the priory remains.

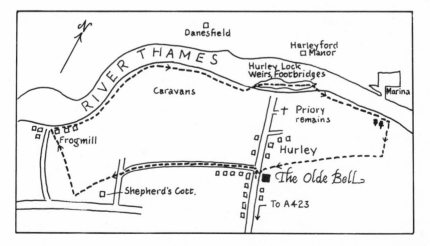

The Walk

Cross the High Street from The Olde Bell to walk down Shepherd's Lane, a quiet, leafy little road past pleasant houses and wide fields. At the crossroads follow the path opposite and walk past the side of Shepherd's Cottage alongside the hedge. Follow the path across the field to the road with wide views of the Grassland Research Station, property of the Agricultural Research Council, on the left. Turn right at the hedge to follow a marked path across the middle of the field to a stile. Go over the stile and carry on along the path behind the gardens of some riverside houses; go over another stile and cross a garden to reach the towpath alongside the river. Turn right onto it and follow the bank for a good mile past houses, fields and a large group of holiday bungalows and caravans set well back behind a hedge. Ducks and geese waddle about the bank and retreat in an unruly huddle at the sight of a large dog. Not so the swans who will threaten the dog if it should dare to enter the water. The huge Gothic pile of Danesfield Manor dominates the skyline above the opposite bank. After another mile the towpath narrows close to the bank and proceeds over a wooden footbridge to Hurley Lock. Walk the full length of the lock to re-cross the river by an identical bridge 100 yards past it. Turn left to follow the towpath with Harleyford Manor and its marina and caravan site on the opposite bank. Go through a pedestrian gate and, 100 yards or so on from this, take a marked right hand path through a little brake. There is another wooden footbridge about 100 yards ahead on the towpath; if you've got to it you've gone too far!

At the end of the path a T junction is reached. Turn right here and follow the path over the flat riverside meadows, crossing a lane by caravans to a marked path opposite. The path emerges onto Hurley High Street just to the right of The Olde Bell. Cross the road to find the car park.

Marlow
The Cross Keys

The town of Marlow is probably most famous for its graceful suspension bridge with its twin towers spanning a broad loop of the river Thames above a roaring weir. It is a charming small riverside town with some very fine and well cared-for buildings of the 18th and 19th centuries in the High Street. The Cross Keys in Spital Street is a 1935-built pseudo-Tudor edifice, not particularly preposessing to look at but the welcome, once inside, is gratifying. It has one long bar-room, plainly furnished with wooden-backed Windsor chairs and tables and the well-stocked bar is raised a little above floor level. All the food on the premises is home-cooked and prepared and there is a tremendous menu of bar snacks, both hot and cold, and all at astoundingly reasonable prices. The menu of hot meals on the blackboard changes every day and includes beef curry, steak and kidney pie, mixed grills and fish. Snacks include fresh rolls, brown or white, filled with a choice of fifteen varieties of meat, fish, cheese and salad and delicious, piping hot toasted sandwiches. Two real ales are sold: Courage Best and Courage Directors. One red and two white

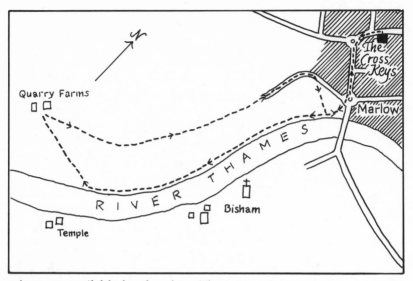

wines are available by the glass. There is a pleasant patio area at the back with wooden benches and tables.

Opening times are from 11 am to 3 pm and 6 pm to 11 pm on weekdays. Sunday hours are 12 noon to 3 pm and 7 pm to 10.30 pm. Telephone: 0628 482522.

How to get there: The Cross Keys is in Spital Street at the top of Marlow's High Street – the other end from the bridge.

Parking: Typical of the pubs in Marlow, this one has no car park, but there are two large Pay & Display car parks very nearby. In fact The Cross Keys backs onto the park off Liston Road, which is a turning on the left if Marlow is approached from the M40 slip-road from High Wycombe. On the right, just further on and at a roundabout, is a large car park exactly opposite the pub. The alternative to these is to park in the huge car park on the right at the roundabout at the bridge end of the High Street. Walk back up the High Street, an opportunity to admire the architecture, and turn right at the top to find The Cross Keys after 200 yards or so.

Length of the walk: 4 miles. Map: OS Pathfinder 1157 (GR 850863).

A flat walk for a good mile along the river bank south of Marlow, passing lovely Bisham church casting its calm reflection in the water, and back to the town by way of water meadows.

106

The Walk

Turn left out of The Cross Keys and left again into the High Street and follow it to a roundabout within sight of the river bridge. Cross here to the tall metal gates and take the footpath across the grass to the towpath alongside the river. Follow the path for a good mile passing the lovely old building of Bisham church on the opposite bank. Also opposite is Bisham Abbey, now a centre for adult physical recreation training. The abbey is interesting for the diversity of its architecture and the quaint clock tower above the stables.

Cross several footbridges over small feeder streams and soon the rather grand houses and marina next to Temple Lock can be seen on the left bank. There are wide views of the tree-clad Chilterns on the right. Just before the lock turn right onto an obvious track and follow it ahead through a green metal gate. Go past the farmhouse of Quarry Farms and take the grass path on the right. Follow this path for about ¾ mile alongside the flat water meadows; it is here that pheasants can often be seen in the autumn. The comfortable red-brick houses of some of the more prosperous Marlow residents are dotted among the trees away to the left. There are glimpses of Bisham church and the abbey through the raggedy hedge on the right.

After ¾ mile go over a stile onto a narrow lane leading back into Marlow. After a further ½ mile there is a gap in the wooden fence on the right leading onto a little path and then over the football field and back, either to the riverside car park or to the river itself by turning right onto the gravel path to follow it to the towpath and thence back to the High Street.

Cookham Dean
Uncle Tom's Cabin

Until the reign of George III Cookham Dean was part of the Royal Manor of Cookham. It was in 1843, when it had been sold by its royal patron, that a Mrs Vansittart, so dismayed by the vice and ignorance of its inhabitants, obtained Parliamentary permission to enclose a piece of common land for the purpose of building a church. The church of St. John the Baptist is at the centre of this small but prosperous settlement on the escarpment overlooking the Thames between Marlow and Bisham. The magnificent sweep of valley and hill landscape from the summit of Winter Hill is famous and Quarry Wood, lying below it and alongside the river, is reputed to be the home of Ratty from 'The Wind in the Willows'.

The popular Uncle Tom's Cabin is of 18th century origin and started life as a brewery/alehouse. Its exterior is unassuming but the heavily timbered and low-ceilinged interior is welcoming and attractive. There are three bars, furnished with cushioned banquettes, tables and chairs and with fires on colder days in two of them. Children are permitted in the bar next to the large and pleasant garden behind the pub where barbecues are prepared on fine summer evenings.

The menu is comprehensive with starters of home-made soup and crusty bread, garlic bread and mushrooms in garlic, as examples. Main courses of delicious cheese and herb topped cottage pie, steak and kidney pie with Guinness, fish dishes and a marvellous melange of vegetables with a breadcrumb and cheese top appear with other 'specials' on a blackboard by the main bar. An interesting variation on a usual theme is the winter ploughman's lunch which includes home-made soup.

Apart from the well-kept Benskins Best Bitter, Gale's of Horndean Bitter and HSB, there is a weekly change of the 'guest' ale and a very good selection of fine malt whiskies. Wines, an excellent house red and two white wines, are sold by the glass.

The inn is open from 11 am to 3 pm, and 5.30 pm to 11 pm on weekdays. Sunday hours are 12 noon to 3 pm and 7 pm to 10.30 pm.

Telephone: 0628 3339.

How to get there: Through Cookham village to the west is Cookham Rise and Cookham Dean is found by taking a signposted turn uphill from this road. The Uncle Tom's Cabin is on the left on a bend about 1 mile up the lane.

Parking: There is adequate car parking space on weekdays but at weekends you may need to park in the lane opposite.

Length of the walk: 2 miles. Map: OS Pathfinder 1157 (GR 877854).

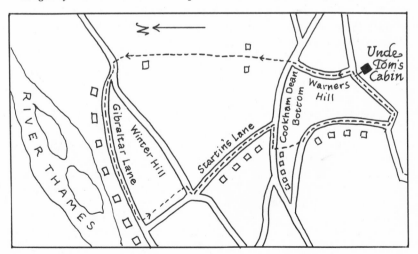

This is quite a short walk but filled with magnificent uphill and downhill views of farmland, orchards and riverside scenery. Some of the climbs are quite steep but the vistas from the top make them very worthwhile.

The Walk

Cross the road outside the pub into Warners Hill and walk gently downhill to the main road. Cross the road to the footpath opposite and follow it uphill through cherry orchards whose blossom is a spectacular sight in springtime and go straight ahead over a stile into a grass field. On the far side of the field, cross a drive and going ahead to a narrow road, cross it into Gibraltar Lane. Follow the lane for almost a mile with woodland on the left and glimpses of the river through the handsome, manicured gardens of the splendid properties on the right. The outskirts of Marlow are visible across the valley, as are the gravel workings now used for waterskiing and other leisure pursuits. Now and again the Marlow Donkey bustles along the single-track rail by the river, hooting importantly as it goes. Peewits and sparrow-hawks can be seen around the meadows close to the river bank.

After about a mile the lane deteriorates into a gravelly path and divides. Just before this division turn left and forge ahead steeply uphill on the grassy sward of Winter Hill. At the top of the hill, take time to stop and look back to drink in the splendid panorama stretching from Bourne End to Bisham. Follow the road at the top to Startin's Lane on the left and follow this narrow little lane steeply downhill again to the main road at Cookham Dean Bottom. Cross the road and follow the lane to the right for a few yards and, just past Hillstone Cottage, turn left onto a bridleway and left again on to a lane after a few yards. Follow this lane uphill to a junction at a triangle of grass where bear left again, signposted Cookham Rise. The Uncle Tom's Cabin is about 50 yards ahead on the right.

Little Marlow
The King's Head

Little Marlow is a small hamlet midway between Marlow and Bourne End off the A4155. Opposite the church of St. John the Baptist is a 16th century Manor House set in 140 acres of grounds which were, in earlier centuries, the property of royalty. In the 12th century a small Benedictine nunnery was established by the river toward Spade Oak ferry and it was one of the smallest religious houses in the country. However, even it did not escape suppression in 1536. Many of the present houses were once shops; a baker, a butcher's shop, a blacksmith and farrier and the old slaughter-house – now named 'the Saltings'.

The ceilings and walls of the bars in the charming 16th century King's Head are oak beamed and reflect the warmth of the welcome that greets you as you enter. The bars are large and airy and children are allowed in when accompanied by parents and having food. The extensive and beautifully shady garden is well furnished and, during the summer, barbecues are often sizzling in the corner of the garden. Inside there is a dazzling choice of real ales: Wethered was once a

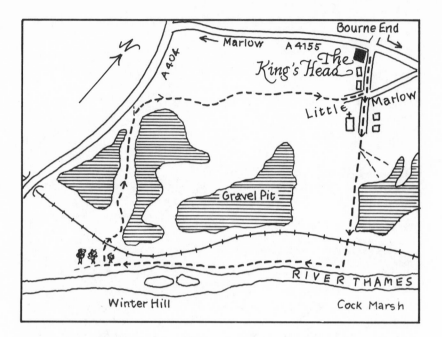

Marlow brewery with an enviable reputation for fine beers and their Bitter is sold; Marston's Pedigree, Boddingtons Best, Abbott Ale and Brakspear Bitter are also available. Wine may be purchased by the glass; red, rosé, and medium and dry whites, and there is a limited but good quality stock of wines by the bottle.

From 12 noon till 2 pm and from 7 pm to 10 pm hot and cold bar meals are served at very reasonable prices – a King's Grill of jumbo sausages, bacon, eggs, mushrooms, and tomato provides a magnificently filling meal, the humble jacket potato comes with no less than seven fillings and the ploughman's lunch includes an apple and salad with a choice of cheeses. Fish dishes are served with crusty bread and salads. There is also a blackboard in the bar listing the day's 'specials'. Opening times are 11 am to 3 pm and 6 pm to 11 pm weekdays. Sunday hours are 12 noon to 3 pm and 7 pm to 10.30 pm.

Telephone: 0628 484407.

How to get there: The King's Head lies between Marlow and Bourne End. It faces a narrow lane, Church Road, on the right of the A4155 about a mile from the roundabout just outside Marlow town.

Parking: There is a car park at the inn.

112

Length of the walk: 4 miles. Map: OS Pathfinder 1157 (GR 873842).

This walk gives you a stroll through the delightful village of Little Marlow and about a mile of towpath with a wooded backdrop (Toad country). The entire route from the end of Church Road is on paths and tracks.

The Walk

Turn right out of the inn yard into the lane and follow it through Little Marlow between a pleasant variety of cottages and houses on either side of the road dating from the 16th to the 19th century and set in colourful gardens behind topiary hedges. There is a handsome dovecote in a garden on the right. The lovely church of St. John the Baptist is of 12th century origin and lies on the right. The footpath to follow is ahead between the church and the vicarage. Follow this shady path and, in about ½ mile cross the railway line which carries the Marlow Donkey between Maidenhead and Marlow. Walk on across the field and turn right to follow the towpath alongside the river. On the opposite bank is Cockmarsh, the home of Toad of Toad Hall. Above it are Winter Hill and Quarry Wood.

After about ¾ mile there is a narrow strip of woodland coming down to the towpath by a small footbridge. Cross the bridge and take the footpath on the right through the copse and away from the river. Cross the railway line again and make a rather wobbly crossing over a makeshift little bridge across a small stream. Large gravel pits can be glimpsed through the trees. The path forks about 100 yards from the main road. Take the right fork here to follow the path alongside the gravel pit. Cross to the other side of the hedge at the public footpath sign. Follow the path/track over three fields and between hedges to emerge onto a tiny lane at the Queen's Head pub. Follow the lane to its junction and turn left to return up the road to the King's Head.

Well End
The Spade Oak

The inn was built in 1887 and was originally called Ye Ferry Hotel, there being at one time a regular ferry service across the river from this point. Now it is called The Spade Oak and there is no ferry! It is a tall, three-storied black and white Victorian building and has an attractive patio area alongside it set with tables and benches and dotted with small shrubs. Children are not permitted in the bar but there is a pleasant family room next to the long bar and a playground outside. The restaurant decor is very 1930s with 'loopy' curtains and heavily-patterned wallpaper. This is not a low-ceilinged country pub by any means but it is extremely popular with local business people at lunchtimes, nonetheless, and always seems to exude a warm and friendly atmosphere.

There is always a good choice of hot food including fish and chicken dishes and always one or two vegetarian meals such as a delicious vegetable lasagne served with crusty bread and a salad garnish or a Stilton and broccoli quiche. Salad platters and sandwiches are also offered and all the food is very reasonably priced. Three real ales, Flowers, Brakspear and Whitbread are sold and there are four house wines sold by the glass.

The inn is open from 11 am to 11 pm Monday to Saturday and on Sundays from 12 noon to 10.30 pm. The bar is shut every day between 3 pm and 4 pm but meals are served all day from 11.30 am to 9.30 pm.

Telephone: 0628 520090.

How to get there: Well End is a group of small old cottages to the west of Bourne End on the A4155 road to Marlow. From Bourne End turn left into Coldmoorholme Lane which is signposted 'Spade Oak' and the inn lies on the left about a mile or so down.

Parking: There is excellent car parking at the inn.

Length of the walk: 2½-3 miles. Map: OS Pathfinder 1157 (GR 884877).

A gentle, shortish walk with about ¾ mile of riverside and several opportunities to watch the variety of birds for whom the water in the peaceful disused gravel pits is home.

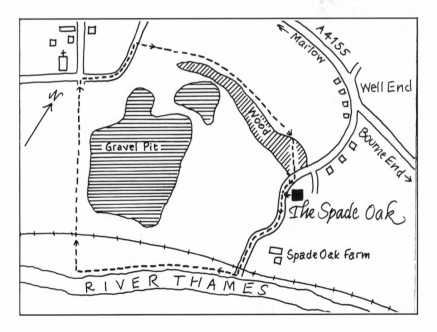

The Walk

Turn left out of the pub and walk towards the river. On the left is the site of a 12th century nunnery which was suppressed in 1536 and nothing now remains of it; in fact the developers are doing a splendid job restructuring the barns and the old farm house which later took its place. Cross over the level crossing to the river; one is exhorted to 'Stop, Look and Listen' advisedly as the little Marlow Donkey plies to and fro very regularly along this strip of railway line. Turn right to walk alongside the river for about ¾ mile. Notice, among the bungalows on the opposite bank, one with a metal balcony in which designs of fish and water birds have been amusingly incorporated. While the hills on the right slope gently away from the river, the abrupt scarp slope of Winter Hill on the left provides a sharp contrast.

After walking over two fields and through two gates turn right past the second gate to walk alongside the hedge to a gate and another railway crossing. Cross the line to the gate on the far side and follow the track ahead. On the right is a broad expanse of water; the gravel pits are now disused and provide a home to a variety of water birds who make their nests on the wooded islets in the middle of the water. The scene is peaceful at all times of the year.

Follow this path for about another ¾ mile to a crossroads. Turn right onto a concrete road and follow it to another junction having skirted the works of the more recently excavated gravel pits. Cross the road to take a marked path opposite over fields with woodland on the right and, soon, the busy gravel workings on the left. About 30 yards from the lane and houses, bear off right into the wood to follow a path to the lane. Turn right onto it to follow it back to The Spade Oak inn.

Cookham
The Crown Inn

The Crown, shrouded gloriously in summer in a thick carpet of scarlet creeper, lies just off Cookham Moor only a few yards from the quaint village of Cookham. The inn was burnt down twice; once in the 1920s and a second time in the 1930s. Very fortunately the Fire Station was situated just behind the inn in Berries Road so the firemen were quickly on the scene though not quickly enough to prevent the building being gutted so that it had to be entirely rebuilt.

This welcoming pub is open 'all day, every day'. There is a large L-shaped bar inside, tables and benches in the front facing the splendid view of the tree-edged moor and the wooded hills of Cookham Dean beyond and a garden at the rear with facilities for children. An enormous blackboard on the wall of the bar lists the menu of the day, a daunting variety of dishes. There are chicken dishes, scampi, fish and chips as well as the humble but filling ham and eggs, very generous and imaginatively served salads with beef, cheese or pâté, ploughman's lunches and imaginatively filled jacket potatoes. To cap all this there is a wicked assortment of desserts and ice-cream.

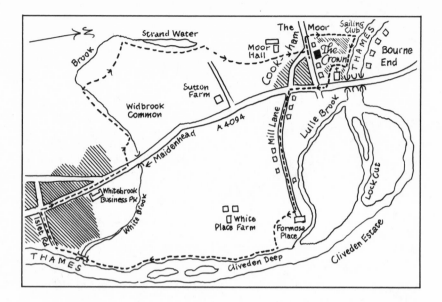

The house serves three real ales: Courage Best and Directors and a guest ale. Five house wines are served by the glass and there is a good, comprehensive wine list. Evening meals are served between 6 pm and 9 pm and lunches from 12 noon. Actual bar opening times are 11 am to 11 pm weekdays and on Sundays, 12 pm to 3pm and 7 pm to 10.30 pm.

Telephone: 0628 520163.

How to get there: Turn left from the A4094 Maidenhead to Bourne End road, just before the church and the river. The Crown Inn is on the right of this road which leads on to Cookham Rise.

Parking: It's a little limited near the pub but there is a free public car park at the far end of the moor and it is only a few minutes walk back to The Crown across the grass.

Length of the walk: 4 miles. Map: OS Pathfinder 1157 (GR 895854).

A walk packed with interest at any time of year: from the activity of Cookham sailing club, through the churchyard with all its connections with Stanley Spencer to the riverside and views of the Cliveden estate.

118

The Walk

Turn right out of the pub and take a step-stile on the right just past a pair of cottages. Walk down the field, crossing the track to the sailing club, and onto the footpth which leads, in only a few yards, to the river where turn right onto the towpath. Follow the river path for a short time and then turn right again onto another path alongside an impressive white Victorian mansion and into the churchyard where the artist, Stanley Spencer, is buried. In the old and beautiful church of the Holy Trinity is a well-executed copy of Spencer's painting of the *Last Supper* and the original cartoon is framed and hanging near it.

At the far side of the churchyard is Churchgate, a small square. Turn left here and then, almost at once, right into the main road. Cross the top of the High Street to the Stanley Spencer Gallery opposite and walk on down Sutton Road for about 100 yards to a crossroads. Turn left down Mill Lane and follow it between comfortable houses set back in orderly gardens for about ½ mile until Formosa Place is reached. From here on the road is private but there is a footpath to the right which runs for a further ½ to ¾ mile through scrubby woodland parallel with the drive and emerges finally at the riverside opposite the Cliveden estate.

Turn right here to follow the towpath for a little over a mile past mysterious tree-clad islands in midstream and over a small footbridge by the impressive Islet Park House. Immediately on the right is a path leading into Islet Road. Follow this for about ¾ mile to the crossroads at the main road. Cross the road to the pavement on the far side and walk past pleasant houses on the left and, shortly, the stark blue-glass Whitebrook Business Park, on the right. Just past a 'Road Narrows' sign, take a stile on the left into Widbrook Common. Cross the common to the brook and then, following its course on the right hand side, walk up the field to a wooden footbridge over the stream. Cross the bridge and continue ahead with the hedge on the left to a stile. Cross this to continue along the well-defined path to another small wooden footbridge over Strand Water. Turn right to follow the path on the nearside of and alongside the stream, crossing the beautiful lime avenue leading to Sutton Farm to the stile opposite. Cross this stile and follow the path to another, then cross this to continue on the path with the high brick wall of Moor Hall on the left and gardens on the right. The path comes out onto the road exactly opposite The Crown. Cross the road with care to reach the car.

Hedgerley
The Brickmould

The Brickmould's present building is fairly modern but a Brickmould public house has existed here since 1753. In 1898 Wellers, the brewers of Amersham, purchased the inn for £1,000. In 1944, Benskins of Watford, who had earlier bought the inn, purchased a plot of land to the rear on which stood three cottages, later demolished. The present building erected subsequently on the site is now wisteria-clad and attractively established. The landlord and his wife offer a warm welcome, the loan of leaflets of circular walks in the area and a 'History of Hedgerley' compiled by the local history society.

There is always a guest ale on sale in the bar as well as four other real ales: Tetley Bitter, Benskins, Burton Ale and Wychwood Best. There is a pleasant outdoor space with a playing area for children who are also welcomed in the 'snug' under adult supervision. All the food is specially prepared to order and there is a daily 'specials' menu on a blackboard in the bar. A great variety of sandwiches are on offer, plentifully garnished with salad. Open prawn sandwiches included almost half a pint of prawns. Hot foods include burgers, steaks, mixed grills, fish dishes and jacket potatoes with a range of fillings.

The inn is open from 11 am to 2.30 pm and 5.30 pm to 11 pm on weekdays. On Saturdays it stays open to refresh all comers (including tired walkers) from 11 am to 11 pm and on Sundays the hours are 12 noon to 3 pm and 7 pm to 10.30 pm.

Telephone: 0753 642716.

How to get there: Hedgerley is signposted off the A355 Windsor to Beaconsfield road, to the east above Farnham Common. Follow the lane to the village, turning left when the One Pin Inn is reached to find The Brickmould ½ mile further along on the left.

Parking: Park just off the road, opposite the pub.

Length of the walk: 3½ miles. Map: OS Pathfinder 1157 (GR 968874).

Enjoy this wooded ramble at any time of year; each season will give it a different aspect.

The Walk

Turn right out of the pub and walk along Kiln Lane past the Memorial Hall on the right and on to a group of cottages amongst which is one called, for unknown reasons, 'Casualty Cottage'. Cross Andrew Hill Lane to the bridlepath opposite and follow it past undulating countryside on the left and the view obscured by a high hedge on the right to Pennlands Farm. Cross the farmyard to go straight ahead on a metalled track winding gently uphill between overhanging trees. On

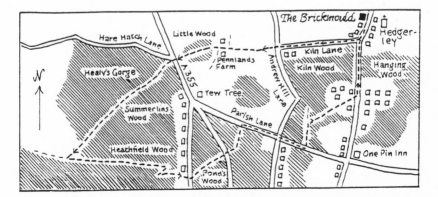

reaching the main road, cross carefully to a marked footpath on the far side on the left corner of Hare Hatch Lane. Go straight ahead over the stile and then, keeping to the left fork, walk through Summerlins Wood, a mixed woodland predominantly of conifer and birch but with some beech and sycamore too. Soon open country appears on the right. At a cross-path re-enter the wood by the path on the left. Notice, alongside the path, huge anthills made up of macerated leaf-mould, bark and pine needles: some are quite two feet high.

Walk past a group of council houses, now 'privatised' and renovated and a black and white house leading onto a lane. Cross the lane to the footpath opposite and follow it through Pond's Wood turning right into Parish Lane. Go across the crossroads and, after 200 yards, take the marked path on the left. After about 30 yards a Y junction is reached. Keep right here and, ignoring all side turnings, stay with the well-defined path ahead, crossing a broad track to a path between fences, and across to the path opposite onto a road. Turn left at the road and walk downhill to find the pub at the bottom.

Dorney
The Palmer Arms

The name Dorney is said to be a derivation from the Saxon 'Island of Bees' and the village has, since Domesday, been famous for its honey. It lies in the centre of a broad Thames valley flood plain, hence the 'island' part of the name. The fields used to flood regularly in winter! The right to graze cattle on the common goes back to feudal days and cattle still meander about the unenclosed pasture. Cattle grids protect the village from unwanted incursions.

The Palmer Arms has been a public house since the 18th century. Since then it has been renovated and much enlarged and its interior has a pristine, crisp, modern look with round whitewood tables and chairs, a large U-shaped bar and a small 'snug' at the front. There are a great number of amusing prints on the walls and the usual 'white lady' haunts bedrooms upstairs, though she has not been apparent of late. Spotless, well-appointed 'offices' lead off the snug. Children are welcomed but no dogs are permitted inside. There is a long, well-furnished garden with bright herbaceous borders and a play area for children. This very busy and popular pub is a free house. A number of real ales are served, among them Palmers Traditional, Wethered, Tetley and Brakspear Bitters and a guest ale, changed monthly. Three house wines are available (very generously) by the glass and there is a full wine list.

The menu is enormous and covers blackboards around the bar and opposite it. Garlic bread and jacket potatoes, ploughman's lunches and filled rolls all feature on the 'snack' board, as do soft herring roes served piping hot in a lemon and butter sauce with a generous chunk of granary bread, and pasta twirls in a creamy cheese sauce. There are imaginative main dishes such as Tandoori lambs' kidneys, chicken supreme and grilled gammon and, on Tuesdays, fish fresh from Billingsgate is cooked in interesting and unusual ways. There is also a variety of inexpensive vegetarian dishes.

The inn is open from 11 am to 3 pm and 6 pm to 11 pm on weekdays. Sunday hours are 12 noon to 3 pm and 7 pm to 10.30 pm.

Telephone: 0628 666612.

How to get there: Dorney is on the B3026 Eton to Maidenhead road. The Palmer Arms is on the right after the signposted turning, on the left, to Boveney.

Parking: There is a large car park at the pub.

Length of the walk: 2½-3 miles. Map: OS Pathfinder 1173 (GR 932791).

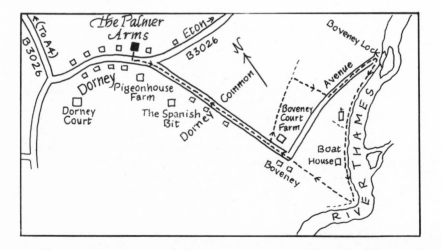

An easy walk across Dorney common to the river at Boveney, with Windsor Castle in the distance. Combine with a visit to Dorney Court during the summer months.

The Walk

Turn left out of the pub and walk through the village, between some delightful timbered 15th to 16th century houses and cottages, to the common. Cross the road at Pigeonhouse Farm and, after about 100 yards, take the narrow lane on the right signposted Boveney. Go over the common past a riding-school called 'The Spanish Bit' and some pleasantly substantial houses in well-groomed gardens. Cattle graze quietly over the pasture and Windsor Castle dominates the skyline away to the left. In summer and spring the grassland is made colourful by hundreds of wild flowers, tiny pink crane's-bill, buttercups and meadowsweet. Later tall thistles with huge blue heads appear and the land is alive with swallows, swooping and diving across it in quick, darting flight.

Just before a Road Narrows sign turn left to follow a path alongside a ditch to a stile. Go over the stile and follow the marked path ahead, bearing left on to a wider path behind the farm buildings after about 100 yards, and on through the flat water meadows. At a T junction turn right onto a path alongside a small brake of trees on the right. At the field edge turn left onto a lane leading to Boveney Lock, a marvellous avenue of horse chestnut trees whose beautiful candles of blossom are a delight in springtime. Turn right at the lock to follow the towpath with the broad, tranquil river flowing by on the left. Soon a tiny flint and stone church is reached; this little chapel of St. Mary Magdalene was most probably used by rivermen as a place of worship when there were large, busy wharves nearby used for the loading and shipment of timber from Windsor forest. It is worth a little diversion here to take the narrow path beside the church to the lane on which stands Boveney Court. Two rampant stone lions guard the gates before this beautiful warm red-brick Tudor manor. It is an E-shaped house of substantial size; once the property of Burnham Abbey, it is now a private residence.

Return to the towpath to walk past a large boathouse and then, after about another ⅓ of a mile, turn right onto a path opposite a group of houses and a Tudor tower. Follow the narrow path over the field and straight ahead onto the lane across Dorney common again and turn left at Pigeonhouse Farm to find the Palmer Arms on the right.

Eton Wick
The Pickwick

Since its foundation in 1440, Eton college has had a profound effect on the small community of Eton Wick: the Provost was, at one time, Rector and the College chapel was Eton Wick's parish church and the college provided a good deal of employment locally. In the 19th century Eton College, as tithe owners of much of the land, supported the villagers in their opposition to the Enclosure Bill which John Penn, the then Lord of the Manor, tried to push through Parliament. The villagers won their case and keep their Common and Lammas land in perpetuity as, in 1965, the land was registered under the Commons Registration Act so that it would need another Act of Parliament to release the land for development. Eton Wick will never be built over!

The Pickwick was built around 1840 and, in 1842, became a beer house. The original beer retailer, William Simmons, doubled up as local carpenter, builder and coal merchant. Young's brewery bought the licence in this century. The pub has won a brewery award, taking third place in a competition between all the Young's pubs for 'front of house' appearance and its very pleasant patio area at the back. The attractively beamed bar and its horse brasses, deep red plush banquettes and dark wooden furniture with, on cold days, a 'log' fire at both ends create a warm and friendly atmosphere and the pub is very popular locally, especially at lunchtimes. Children are permitted in the bar in the care of an adult. There is unobtrusive piped music and one interesting feature for sale is a rack of bags of locally grown culinary herbs – dozens of them!

Much of the food is inspired home-cooked Malaysian: the curries are unusual, hot but not burning and having a delicate spicy after-taste. Especially good is the curried chicken, an enormous helping with a mound of saffron rice and a side salad. Then there are the traditional English meals like steak and kidney pie and fish and chips or sausage and egg, all reasonably priced. The extensive menu which also includes the usual snacks is on a blackboad over the bar. Young's draught bitters, Best and Special, are sold and white wines, medium and dry, are available by the glass. There is an impressive array of spirits behind the bar including some of the rarer malt whiskies.

Opening times are from 11.30 am to 2.30 pm Monday to Friday (until 3 pm on Saturday) and on Sunday from noon to 3 pm. The pub is open every evening from 5.30 pm to 11 pm.

Telephone: 0753 861713.

How to get there: Turn off the A4 from Maidenhead to follow Lake End Road (the B3026), signposted for Dorney and Eton. Go through Dorney and over the broad expanse of common to Eton Wick village. The Pickwick is on the left hand side.

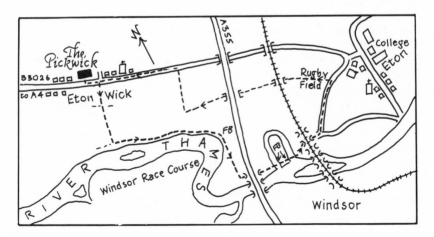

Parking: Car parking space is limited at the pub but road parking is easy and not obtrusive.

Length of the walk: 2½ -3 miles. Map: OS Pathfinder 1173 (GR 951784).

A fascinating stroll along the river bank and close by Eton college chapel. Magnificent views of Windsor Castle dominate the skyline for much of the route.

The Walk

Turn left out of the pub and cross the road to take the marked path on the right following it, over a bridleway, to the towpath alongside the river. Turn left to follow the broad, clean path toward Windsor and Eton. There is a fine view of Eton College chapel ahead and, on the right, the river flows peacefully. Soon Windsor Race Course appears on the right. Follow the path over a pretty wooden footbridge and on to the arch beneath the busy A355. On the far side of the arch the path becomes the Windsor and Eton cycle path: remember that bicycles don't make any noise when they come up behind you! From here there is a marvellous view of Windsor Castle against the skyline.

Go over two metal footbridges and, after the second, immediately turn left onto the path which leads to the railway arches. It is a daunting thought that all that brickwork in front of one, forming all those arches, was put there simply so that Queen Victoria could get to Windsor by train via Slough. Go under the railway arch and turn right to follow the metalled track to a T junction, then turn left onto a lane. On the right the castle, the magnificent St. George's chapel and the castle keep are now plainly visible high above the surrounding landscape and the town.

Just before a modern green-roofed building take a marked path on the left through a recreation ground and then straight across a rugby field and on under the railway again at a marked footpath sign. Follow the bridleway ahead, under the A355, and then about 100 yards on the far side, turn right onto a footpath towards the road. Cross the road to the footway and turn left to return to The Pickwick. It is possible to go on along the last bridleway and return to the pub by the original footpath but the horses tend to churn up the clayey mud and it can be very heavy walking, so the short distance along the road was chosen as an alternative.